AMBROSIA

Jyoti Das was born in Shillong. Her other works include *Aponar Akhilot Chinese Byanjon* and *Manxhar Vividh Byanjon*. She also writes food columns, short stories and articles for various magazines like *Nandini, Xadin, Parijat* and *Prantik* in Assam.

Her social activities have taken her to different pockets of Assam where she got the opportunity to pick up the finer nuances of Assamese cuisine. At present, she is working as a volunteer teacher at Sishu Saratha, a school for spastic students in Guwahati.

For more information, log on to www.assamesecuisines.com.

AMBROSIA
...From the Assamese Kitchen

Jyoti Das

RUPA

Published by
Rupa Publications India Pvt. Ltd 2008
7/16, Ansari Road, Daryaganj
New Delhi 110002

Sales centres:
Allahabad Bengaluru Chennai
Hyderabad Jaipur Kathmandu
Kolkata Mumbai

Copyright © Jyoti Das 2008

Foreword copyright © Victor Banerjee 2006

Photograph by Aanzan and Jyoti Das

All rights reserved.
No part of this publication may be reproduced, transmitted, or stored in a retrieval system, in any form or by any means, electronic, mechanical, photocopying, recording or otherwise, without the prior permission of the publisher.

ISBN: 978-81-291-1374-0

Fourth impression 2018

10 9 8 7 6 5 4

The moral right of the author has been asserted.

Typeset in Palatino by Mindways Design, New Delhi

Printed at Repro Knowledgecast Limited, Thane

This book is sold subject to the condition that it shall not, by way of trade or otherwise, be lent, resold, hired out, or otherwise circulated, without the publisher's prior consent, in any form of binding or cover other than that in which it is published

*This book is dedicated to
Raji, Rakhee, Rasween and Ronku
for their support and encouragement*

From the Author's Desk...

I had the privilege of spending a part of my life in Upper Assam, in Duliajan and Moran, thanks to my conjugal life that required us to move from one place to another. My interaction with people from different spheres during my stay in these places, especially in Moran, motivated my interest in cooking and the kitchen culture of my state. I would like to take this opportunity to thank the people of Moran for inspiring me and showering me with their unconditional love and affection.

This book would have been incomplete without the unwavering support from my husband Mr Ashok Das. I would like to thank Mr Victor Banerjee for his encouragement and help during the endeavour. I must mention Mr Pradip Acharyya's interest and guidance that facilitated this effort of mine. I also thank my sister-in-law Mrs Sarbari Saikia and my daughter-in-law Rasween, whose moral support from time to time meant so much. A special mention would be my nephew Trisham, who helped me while I dealt with Microsoft for my work. My heartiest thanks would go to Rahul Bhuyan for organising the book. Finally, this effort would not have progressed beyond a dream, if not for my children Raji and Rakhee who worked on my weak points and made the final output look the way it is.

Contents

Acknowledgements   *xix*
Foreword by Victor Banerjee   *xxi*
About Assam   *xxviii*

Assamese Cuisine   1

Pithas   3
Kholasapori Pitha
Rice Pancake   5
Til Pitha
Sesame Pancake   6
Ghila Pitha
Fried Pancake   8
Narikolor Bhoja Pitha
Fried Coconut Pitha   9
Phula Pitha
Puffed Pitha   10
Kol Pitha-1
Banana Pitha-1   12
Kol Pitha-2
Banana Pitha-2   13
Poka Mithoi
Rice Powder And Jaggery Balls   15
Tekeli Pitha
Pitcher Cake (sweet)   17
Tekeli Pitha
Pitcher Cake (savoury)   18
Anguli Pitha
Finger-like Pitha   20

Aam Aru Bora Chaulor Pitha
Mango and Sticky Rice Pitha   22
Narikolor Laru
Coconut Ladoo   24
Kathali Seppa
Carambola   25

Chaul (Rice)   27
Baanhor Chungat Bora Chaul
Sticky Rice in a Bamboo Hollow   31
Chunga Chaul
Rice in a Bamboo Hollow   33
Baanhor Chungat Kharisa Diya Bhat
Fermented Bamboo Shoot Rice in a Bamboo Hollow   35

Bor/ Pakoras (Fritters)   37
Rongalao Phulor Bor
Pumpkin Flower Fritters   39
Sewali Phulor Bor
Coral Jasmine Pakoras   40
Mosmosiya Bengena Bhoja
Cruncy Brinjal Fritters   41
Maachor Konir Bor
Fish Egg Pakoras   42
Masur Dailor Bor
Red Lentil Pakoras   44

Khar (Alkali)   45
Amitar Khar
Papaya Khar   47
Sanmehali Kharor Lagot Kathal Guti
Mixed Khar with Jackfruit Seeds   49
Mati Dailor Khar
Black Gram Khar   51
Masur Dail Aru Baahgajor Khar

Red Lentil and Bamboo Shoot Khar 52
Sajina Pator Khar
Drumstick Leaves Khar 54
Sajinar Khar
Drumstick Khar 56
Posolar Khar
Banana Stem Khar 58
Xaakor Khar
Herbs Khar 60

Chutney 63
Kharoli
Fermented Mustard Powder with Alkali 65
Pani Tenga
Fermented Mustard Powder with a Souring Agent 66
Kharisa
Fermented Bamboo Shoot 67
Kesa Amar Chutney
Raw Mango Chutney 68
Podinar Chutney
Mint Chutney 69
Konbilahir Chutney
Cherry Tomato Chutney 70
Amlokhir Chutney
Amla (Indian Gooseberry) Chutney 71

Dail (Lentil) 73
Aada Diya Mogur Dail
Moong Daal with Crushed Ginger 75
Fola Mogur Dail
Split Green Gram with the Skin 76
Masur Dailot Outenga
Red Lentil with Elephant Apple 77
Mati Dailor Lagot Outenga
Black Gram with Elephant Apple 79
Butor Dailor Lagot Kharisa

Bengal Gram with Fermented Bamboo Shoot   81
Arahor Dailor Lagot Sajina Pat
Yellow Gram with Drumstick Leaves   82
Maachar Muri Ghonto
Fish Head with Moong Daal   84

Vegetables   87
Dhekia Patot Diya
Dhekia Baked in a Banana Leaf   89
Khutura Bhaji
Fried Green Calalu   91
Methi Xaak Aru Alu Bhaji
Fenugreek Leaves with Potatoes   92
Patot Diya Tengesi Xaak
Roasted Indian Sorrel   93
Bhatot Diya Kolmou Xaak
Swamp Cabbage and Rice   94
Sajina Phul Aru Haanh Koni Bhaji
Drumstick Flowers with Duck Eggs   95
Sarioh Botar Lagot Sajina
Drumstick with Mustard Seed Paste   96
Labra Bhaji
Mixed Vegetables   97
Pur Diya Tetakerela
Stuffed Bittergourd   99
Bilahi Aru Haanh Koni Bhaji
Fried Tomatoes with Duck Eggs   102
Kathalor Torkari
Jackfruit Curry   103
Alu Dom
Potato Curry   105
Jatilao Bhaji
Fried Bottlegourd   107
Rangalao Bhaji

Fried Pumpkin	108
Alu Koni Pitika	
Mashed Potatoes and Eggs	109
Bengena Pitika	
Mashed Brinjal	110
Manxo (Meat/Poultry)	**111**
Patha Manxor Jhul	
Mutton Curry	113
Shanmehali Xaakor Lagot Patha Manxo	
Mutton with Mixed Herbs	115
Patha Manxor Korma	
Mutton Korma	117
Baanhgajor Lagot Kukura	
Chicken with Bamboo Shoot	119
Paleng Xaakot Kukura	
Chicken with Spinach	121
Jalukia Kukura	
Chicken with Pepper	123
Kukurar Lagot Ada	
Chicken with Ginger	124
Rasal Kukura	
Juicy Chicken	125
Kumura Aru Haanh	
Duck Curry with White Pumpkin	127
Bhoja Haanh	
Duck Fry	129
Paro Manxor Jhul	
Pigeon Curry	130
Phola Mati Dailor Lagot Gahori	
Pork with Split Black Gram	132
Pithagurir Lagot Gahori Manxo	
Pork with Rice Powder	134
Baanhgajor Lagot Gahori	
Pork with Bamboo Shoot	135

Maach (Fish) — 137
Pitha Gurir Lagot Sijua Maach
Boiled Fish with Rice Powder — 139
Kharisar Rasot Bhoja Magur Maach
Cat Fish Fried in Bamboo Shoot Juice — 140
Maachor Kalia
Fish Kalia — 142
Maach Pitika
Mashed Fish — 144
Bhapot Diya Elihi Maach
Steamed Hilsa Fish — 145
Baanhor Chungat Maach
Fish in a Bamboo Hollow — 146
Patot Dia Maach – 1
Baked Fish in a Banana Leaf – 1 — 148
Patot Dia Dorikona Maach – 2
Baked Fish In Banana Leaf – 2 — 150
Sukan Maachor Gura
Grinded Dry Fish — 152
Kosu Pator Lagot Saru Maach
Small Fish with Colocasia Leaves — 153
Outengar Maachor Tenga
Elephant Apple Fish Tenga — 154
Dhekia Aru Bilahir Tenga
Tomato and Dhekia Tenga — 156
Kothal Gutir Lagot Maachor Tenga
Fish Tenga with Jackfruit Seeds — 158
Thekera Aru Alu Tenga
Potato Tenga with Cocum — 160
Narikolor Rosot Maach
Fish with Coconut Juice — 162
Paleng Xaakor Maachor Jhul
Fish Curry with Spinach — 164
Doi Maach
Curd Fish — 166

Narasinghar Lagot Magur Maach
Cat Fish with Curry Leaves   167

My Favourite Dishes   **169**
Tel Phuit Khar   171
Sewali Phulor Khar
Coral Jasmine Khar   172
Mosundari Aru Nohoru
Mosundari with Garlic   174
Kothalguti Pitika
Mashed Jackfruit Seeds   175
Koldil Bhaji
Spadix Fry   176
Kosu Tenga
Sour Colocasia   178
Maachor Petu Bhoja
Fried Fish Guts   180
Kharisar Tenga
Fermented Bamboo Shoot Tenga   182
Pura Goroi Maachor Pitika
Barbequed Fish   184
Adar Jhul
Ginger Curry   185
Magur Maach Aru Bhedailotar Jhul
Cat Fish Curry with King Tonic   187
Xaakor Jhul
Herbs Curry   189
Suklatir Jhul
Suklati Curry   190
Thekerar Maachor Tenga
Fish Tenga with Cocum   193
Sarioh Xaakor Lagot Gahori Manxo
Pork with Mustard Leaves   195
Mur Maar Kukurar Vyanjan
My Mother's Chicken Recipe   197

Kukurar Suruha
Assamese Chicken Soup | 198

Mitha Ahar (Dessert) | **199**
Panilaor Payas
Bottlegourd Payas | 201
Chaulor Payas
Rice Payas | 202
Pithagurir Payas
Rice Powder Payas | 203
Alur Pudding
Potato Pudding | 204
Bhator Payas
Chilled Rice Pudding | 205
Sewair Kheer
Vermicelli Kheer | 206
Cornflouror Mitha Ahar
Cornflour Pudding | 207
Vanilla Custard | 208
Caramel Pudding | 209
Rongalao Aru Paneeror Mitha Ahar
Pumpkin Cheese Cake | 211
Norabogorir Rosot Norabogori
Delicious Peaches in Peach Syrup | 213
Strawberry and Cream | 214
Rongalaor Souffle
Pumpkin Souffle | 215
Phalor Lagot Cream
Fruit and Cream | 217
Baanhor Chungar Pudding
Bamboo Hollow Pudding | 219
Amitar Kheer
Papaya Kheer | 220
Komal Chaulor Payas
Soft Rice Payas | 221

Lutharir Lagot Norabogori
Peaches and Rice Powder Pudding   222

Xaak and *Saatxaaki*   **225**
Assamese Course Meals   **231**
Glossary   **234**
References   **238**

Acknowledgements

I want to extend my heartfelt thanks and appreciation to the following people:

Stj Bhola Nath Saikia
Sjta Bibha Saikia
Sjta Bina Barua
Dr Anil Saikia
Dr Asimava Dutta
Mrs Sangita Agarwal
Mr Biswa Prasad Pegu
Mrs Henguli Bezbarua
Mr Anup Saikia
Mr Pranab Saikia (Raj)

I feel that a cookery book should not just contain recipes. Besides leaving you with mouth-watering flavours and tastes, what one learns from it should bring one's heart and soul closer to the land of the origin of the delicacies.

Foreword

Assam is my private wonderland, my childhood's Disneyland; with all its thrills in the jungles, rides on elephants being charged by rhinos, the swoop of hundreds of wild ducks and geese over the Brahmaputra where the majestic fish eagle fights with giant mahseer to beach them, and hundreds of memories that very few children have the privilege to cherish. I had the best of both worlds; a retreating culture of colonialism with its sophisticated hangovers of shikars and gala Christmas parties on one hand and an introduction to the quiet charm of simple people, on the other. To add masala and a real zing to it all, were the colourful tribes that surrounded the valley and whose children I went to school with.

Today Assam is still largely unspoiled, topographically speaking. But while I am thrilled to see a mud hut that I can recognise from four decades ago, there is a sad consciousness of how time has been allowed to stand still in the lives of simple folk, who still till the soil and toil in the sun and wade through floods to eke out an ordinary, almost meaningless existence. I begin to notice the barrenness created by felled peepals and banyans: there is a silence now where hill mynas once screeched over the flap of imperial pigeons and no red jungle fowl scurry through the brush and sly leopards no longer growl in the midst of descend at dusk upon a land of dead coyotes poisoned by pesticides. So much has changed in the environment and so little had changed in the lives of the poor.

Oil-rich, tea-rich and bamboo-rich, rural Assam has little to show for its wealth.

But this is meant to be an introduction to a cook book! So let me quit dwelling on the tastelessness of social depravation and tell you to sample the mouth-watering opulence that the Assamese lay out on their tables.

Almost every cuisine on the planet is an acquired taste: very few have universal appeal like the Chinese and Indian. The unique aspect of Assamese food is its simplicity and clean tastes. There is a charming rusticity to almost all the recipes. The smells and aromas in the kitchen, when you cook Assamese food, have a primitive charm that is typical and distinctively Assamese.

From the banana to the bamboo, from pigeon to duck, from fascinating flavours produced by ash to desserts smoked in bamboo hollows, the imaginative versatility within the confines and limitations of tribal, rural, agrarian and riverine cultures that peoples the largest valley in the world will astound you.

This book in not one that you will be able to simply pick up and cook from and then expect to enjoy everything you prepare. Wherever you are in the world, I am afraid you will have to first find an Assamese housewife (or man in an apron) whom you will have to befriend, cultivate, flatter and then coax into giving you secrets that each family guards to make almost every single dish in this book special, in an inimitable sort of way. This is the best and the worst thing about most Assamese, in fact almost all the north-eastern food, even from the hills that surround Assam—they all taste subtly different from home to home, from developed regions in Lower Assam to the forested divisions of Upper Assam, from silted banks of the Brahmaputra to the bamboo forests of Nagaland, Mizoram and Arunachal Pradesh.

I am not going to pick up recipes that are my favourites; on the contrary, I shall dive into so many that I had not been privy to before now and open up new horizons for myself so the land I hold so dearly to my heart becomes, for me, a wonderland renewed.

One final tip before I get down to the finger-licking experiences that await you; don't waste time having French, Australian or Napa Valley wines with your Assamese meal. The Assamese are (by and large) not a pretentious people and their down to earth simplicity is never an affectation. Tried and tested, I can recommend a few

Italian Chiantis or a simple buttermilk prepared from homemade curd and then end with a shot of Grappa—never Port and cheese: a Cohiba Havana cigar? Sure.

And please, please all you healthy joggers, treadmill stompers and weight-watchers, don't worry, Assamese food has the least calories and is not fattening.

Happy eating.

Victor Banerjee
Friday, 3 November 2006

About Assam

Assam, which was known as Pragjyotishpura in ancient times, is the gateway to the north-east. Late Hem Barua, a renowned MP from Assam, called it the land of the Red River (Luit) and the Blue Hill (Nilachal). The mighty Brahmaputra, also known as Luit, is the main river of Assam and the only male river in the world. Assam is also home to the famous Kamakhya Temple, which is situated atop the Nilachal hill.

Assam has many places of tourist attraction. In addition to many breathtaking landscapes, it boasts of numerous historical sites, golf courses and wildlife sanctuaries like the Kaziranga and Manas national parks. Kaziranga is home to the world-famous one-horned rhinoceros. Assam also has more than a thousand tea-gardens and is one of the largest manufacturers of tea in the world.

For a nature lover, Assam is home to some precious and endangered species of orchids. Enthralling and mesmerising, there are about three hundred and fifty species of orchids in Assam.

Assam is also rich in natural resources like oil, natural gas and coal. Approximately, it contributes to one tenth of India's total crude oil production. The first oil well in Assam was drilled in 1889 in Digboi, Upper Assam. It was the second well after Titusville in the United States where petroleum was first discovered.

From time immemorial, the people of Assam have been fine craftsmen. Assam's artistically made cane and bamboo products are highly appreciated in the country. Handmade Assamese jewellery are exquisite and the gold used for the ornaments is refined. Brass (*pital*) and bell metal (*kaah*), products of Sarthebari of Lower Assam are famous everywhere for their aesthetic beauty and durability.

Sualkuchi, known as Manchester of Assam, is famous for its *paat* (silk), *muga* (golden buff silk) and *eri* (white silk). This rich Assamese fabric is increasingly becoming designers' delight. *Muga* silk is found only in Assam.

Besides it's wealth of natural resources, wildlife and historical sites, Assam also has a rich culture. The primary festival of Assam is *Bihu*, the agricultural festival which is celebrated by all Assamese people, irrespective of caste, creed or religion. The celebration of the Assamese New Year is known as *Bohag Bihu* which is the sowing time. Bohag also known as *Rongali Bihu*, is the festival of merry-making. This is the time of celebration with songs and the famous *Bihu* dance, the traditional dance form of Assam. *Kati Bihu* marks the completion of sowing and transplantation of paddy. During this season people light diyas in the paddy fields and in their homes. This is to welcome Goddess Lakshmi. *Magh Bihu* in the winter is celebrated at the end of the harvest period. It is a season of plenty, when people feast and engage in fun games like *koni juj* (egg fight), *tekeli bhonga* (pitcher breaking), rowing, bullfights etc.

Assamese Cuisine

The Assamese believe that food is a gift of God and its preparation a form of prayer. A bath and clean clothes are a must before one enters the kitchen. An elaborate ritual marks the preparation of feasts for different occasions like weddings, shradhs and so on; the basic purpose is ritualised cleanliness and hygiene.

There is little awareness about the cuisine of Assam. It is unlikely that one would directly encounter native Assamese cooking, wandering through streets and bazaars in the metropolises around the world. Like the simple Assamese people, the food of Assam is rather simple and bland; with little or no spices at all; yet is delicious. Aromatic herbs add varied flavours to the cuisine, making it simple, yet tasty, wholesome and healthy.

Ginger, garlic, green chillies, pepper, onions etc are generously used. Mustard oil is the preferred cooking medium traditionally; though health considerations are making the urban Assamese move to low cholesterol vegetable cooking oils. The use of *panch phuron* while tempering is very common.

The food of Upper Assam has the influence of communities like the Ahom while lower west Assam has the influence of West Bengal and Bihar. Generous use of mustard seeds and coconut is very common in this area. Bamboo shoot, fresh or fermented, is common in Upper Assam but not so in Lower Assam, except amongst the ethnic groups.

Eating out is becoming a part of the urban lifestyle and various food joints are introducing various Indian, oriental and western cuisines to the urban Assamese. Establishments serving typical Assamese food in traditional Assamese utensils of *kaah* (bel metal), like *thaal* (plates) and *bati* (bowl) are also on the rise. Traditional food is served in several courses. A balanced Assamese diet starts with the weekly purgative *khar* (traditional alkali), rice, pulses, herbs, vegetables and fish *tenga*. The use of medicinal and aromatic herbs are already beginning to draw universal attention.

Food can be served in anything handy, but the flavours of *xaak* and fish steamed and/or roasted wrapped in fresh banana leaves is an entirely different affair.

Pithas

I remember spending the winter vacations with my grandparents in Nagaon, a town in Assam. Our whole family would pack their bags, and come down from Shillong to Nagaon. We would be greeted by huge stacks of paddy in the compound of the house. Accompanied by cousins and my brothers, I would climb the stacks and jump on them for hours. We would get down with bruises and scratches. I was oblivious to the fact that all the jumping on the paddy stacks was in a way, a step towards the preparation of *pithas*.

The importance of *pitha* to Assam can be best summarised by what someone had once famously said, 'Assamese identity is never complete without *pitha*.' *Pitha* is basically a snack made from rice. The main ingredients used for making *pithas* are rice powder, sesame, jaggery and coconut. During the *Magh Bihu* season (January - February), the granaries are overflowing with harvested crops. This is the season of plenty and the time when the ladies of the family are busy preparing varieties of *pithas*.

Bora chaul (sticky rice) is considered to be one of the most valuable ingredients of mother nature for the people of Assam and is used for making certain varieties of *pitha*. There are three varieties of *bora chaul* – white, reddish and black. The black one is used for a light meal and for making *payas*. The reddish one is more popular than the white. But in urban areas, people prefer the white *bora chaul* as it makes the *pithas* look attractive. There is considerable difference in the *pithas* in Upper Assam and Lower Assam. As we move up (Upper Assam), the length of the *pithas* increase and they get thinner. This could be attributed to the fact that the people there use flatter *tawas* (pans) than the ones generally used in Lower

Assam which are concave. Sometimes one would also come across half-moon shaped *til pithas* (sesame), as opposed to the elongated ones, in Lower Assam.

There are wide varieties of *pithas* made with normal and sticky rice. Many delicious *pithas* can also be made without the use of oil, like the *til pitha, tekeli pitha, poka mithoi* and *kol pitha*. If fried, one has to use mustard oil. For different flavours one can also use lemon rind, orange rind or pepper. In addition, fruits like mangoes, bananas, jackfruit, tal and ripe papayas can be mixed with the rice powder to make the *pithas*. The use of banana leaves while baking or steaming gives the *pithas* a more authentic taste.

Kholasapori Pitha
Rice Pancake

As it is made in an earthen plate (*khol*), this particular pancake is called *kholasapori pitha* in Assamese. It is also called *panipitha* as only water (*pani*) is used to make the batter for the pancake.

Ingredients

Rice powder	:	250 gms
Water	:	300 ml
Mustard oil	:	to smear the griddle

Method

§ Make a batter of the rice powder and water.
§ Heat a griddle or tava. Smear it with oil and pour two ladles of batter and spread it like a pancake.
§ Turn over when done and cook the other side.
§ Serve *kholasapori pitha* with jaggery, pickle or mutton curry.

Note: Variation (savoury) – Add 2 tbsps of finely chopped onions, 1 tbsp of chopped coriander leaves, 1 tsp of grated ginger and a beaten egg to the batter. Also add salt to taste. Serve with mint chutney.

Variation (sweet) – Add 2 tbsps of sugar, ½ tsp of grated lemon rind and 2 beaten eggs while making the batter. Instead of water, make the batter with milk.

Til Pitha
Sesame Pancake

What happens when you take some roasted sesame seeds, pounded coarsely, mix it with jaggery and roll it in Assamese style on pita bread made of rice powder? You get the Assamese *til pitha*, the original basic mouth watering Assamese snack. *Til pitha* is referred to as *dukhiyar pitha* since a poor man also makes it with same festive spirit during *Bihu*.

Does not roshogulla remind every Indian of Kolkata? Similarly if a *khar khua Asomiya*, including my son or daughter, comes across some warm *til pithas*, he or she would definitely be reminded of home. If you have not tasted warm *til pithas*, you don't know what you are missing.

Ingredients

Sticky rice	:	500 gms
Black sesame seed (til)	:	250 gms
Jaggery (grated)	:	400 gms
Freshly ground pepper	:	as per taste

Method

- Soak the rice for 3-4 hours. Drain well.
- Pound the rice to a fine powder. Sieve with a very fine sieve.
- Keep it in an airtight container in a compact condition.
- Clean, wash and dry the sesame seeds beforehand.
- Stir fry the dry seeds in small portions in a wok. Once the seeds start to crackle, remove the wok from the fire. Pound coarsely.

- Mix the pounded sesame seeds with grated jaggery and pepper.
- Heat a griddle. Take a handful of rice power and spread thinly on the hot griddle. Sprinkle the sesame and jaggery mixture on the *pitha* and roll the *pitha*.
- Keep it aside for a while on the side of griddle so that the *pithas* are crisp.
- Serve *til pithas* hot.
- Can be stored for 2 weeks. Just before serving, warm the *pithas* in a warm oven for two minutes as hot *til pithas* are simply delicious.

Note: A variation in the filling of the above pitha can also be made. Instead of sesame seeds, use grated coconut fried with sugar.

Ghila Pitha
Fried Pancake

I remember my grandmother making *ghila pithas*. She would make a dough of rice powder, jaggery and water early on the morning of *Magh Bihu* and *Bohag Bihu*. Sometimes she also added bottlegourd or pumpkin to the dough. She would make small balls, flatten them between her soft palms and make *ghilas*. After making the *ghilas*, she would keep them on a *baanhor saloni* (bamboo sieve) and cover them with a banana leaf. When she had made enough for the family, relatives and neighbours, she would deep-fry them in pure fresh mustard oil and keep them on a *kharahi* (bamboo basket) to drain the excess oil.

Ingredients

Rice flour	:	1 kg
Jaggery (grated)	:	500 gms
Warm water	:	1 cup
Mustard oil	:	for frying

Method

§ Put the jaggery into a cup of warm water. Make a smooth paste.
§ Add the rice powder and knead well into to a smooth dough. Keep it aside for 10 minutes.
§ Make small balls. Flatten the balls.
§ Deep-fry till brown on a medium flame.
§ Serve warm.
§ *Ghila pithas* can be stored for a week.

Jumur dance is performed by tea plantation workers.

Narikolor Bhoja Pitha
Fried Coconut Pitha

Easy to make and very tasty, hot fried coconut *pithas* are delicious with a cup of hot tea.

Ingredients

Rice flour	:	2 cups
Grated coconut	:	½ cup
Sugar	:	½ cup
Milk	:	to knead the dough
Oil	:	for frying

Method

- Mix the rice flour, coconut and sugar.
- Pour the milk and knead into a smooth dough.
- Divide the dough into small balls.
- Flatten the balls and deep-fry upon moderate heat till golden brown in colour.
- Best to eat while still hot.
- *Narikolar bhoja pithas* can be stored for 2-3 days.

Sattriya Nitya is a classical dance of Assam.

Phula Pitha
Puffed Pitha

Phula pitha is similar to the *ghila pitha*. It is the inflated version of *ghila pithas* and are like puffs. Instead of a dough, you prepare a batter. Deep-fry the batter by dropping dollops of it into hot mustard oil. Fry them till they are brown. The air mixed with the batter expands when hot, making the *phula pitha phula,* that is puffed up. My mother would stack them in a *kharahi* (bamboo basket). The excess oil would drip out through the basket. After she would keep aside a few for *Agni* (the god of fire) I would eat some while she would be frying them. *Phula pithas* are sweet and really yummy. The sweetness is from the jaggery is mild and the *pithas* are really smooth.

Ingredients

Sticky rice	:	1 cup
Rice	:	3 cups
Grated jaggery	:	1 cup
Water	:	½ cup
Orange rind	:	1 tsp
Mustard oil	:	for deep frying

Method

§ Soak both varieties of rice together for an hour. Drain well.
§ Pound the rice and sieve.
§ Mix the jaggery with water to make a smooth paste.
§ Add the jaggery paste to the rice powder. Sprinkle some orange rind and mix well. Keep it covered in a fridge overnight.

- § Take the mixture out of the fridge two hours before frying.
- § Heat the mustard oil in a karai. With a round spoon, drop a bit of batter in the oil and fry the *pithas* one by one till golden brown upon a medium flame.
- § Relish *phula pithas*, hot or cold, with a cup of hot tea. They can be stored for a week.

The Kaziranga National Park is home to the world's largest population of one-horned rhinos.

Kol Pitha-1
Banana Pitha-1

During the cold winter evenings when we would come down from Shillong to Nagaon to spend our winter holidays with our grandmother, *kol pitha* was one of our favourite tea-time snacks.

Ingredients

Bananas	:	4 medium-sized
Sugar	:	100 gms
Semolina	:	75 gms
Oil	:	for frying the *pithas*

Method

§ Mash the bananas well.
§ Add the sugar and semolina to the mashed bananas and mix.
§ Make small balls and flatten them. Fry upon moderate heat till golden brown.
§ Lay them out on a paper napkin to soak excess oil.
§ Serve hot *kol pitha* with tea.

Note: Ripe jackfruit pulp can also be used for making this *pitha*.

Bagurumba is one of the folk dances of the Bodo community of Assam.

Kol Pitha-2
Banana Pitha-2

The taste of this *kol pitha* takes me back to my childhood days. It was so tasty that though our always grandmother made plenty, we would never be satisfied and would keep asking for more.

Ingredients

Bananas	:	4 medium-sized
Grated jaggery	:	½ cup
Rice powder	:	1 cup
Ground pepper	:	½ tsp
Milk	:	as required
Banana leaves	:	2
Pure ghee	:	½ tsp

Method

§ Mash the bananas well.
§ Mix the bananas, jaggery, rice power, pepper and a little milk. Divide it into two equal portions.
§ Clean the banana leaves. Dry and hold them over a low fire to make the leaves pliable.
§ Grease the leaves with pure ghee and place the mixture in the centre of the leaves and make two parcels.
§ Tie the parcels with strings and bake them over a hot griddle on both sides, one at a time, till done.
§ Unwrap the parcels and serve hot or cold with tea.

§ The *kol pitha* is a delicacy truly enjoyed if broken into small pieces and served with chilled sweet milk during hot summer days.

Note: It is good for young children and is very filling. It can be baked in an oven.

Mising Bihu is a popular festival in the north-eastern part of Assam.

Poka Mithoi
Rice Powder And Jaggery Balls

This is what my son has to say about *poka mithoi*: 'I did not realise the usefulness of this ladoo until I came to stay in a hostel. I knew about it, but had always ignored it for the softer and sweeter *pithas*. *Poka mithoi* is a hard ladoo. I remember my roommate would pop a couple of them at night, drink some water and would go to sleep. He had a very good appetite as he was a state level cricketer. This particular *pitha* would be his midnight snack. He told me that *poka mithoi* was very filling. I learnt the usefulness of it from a Himachali, a resident of Dharamshala!'

The literal meaning of *poka mithoi* is jaggery cooked in water. The more you heat the jaggery, the sticker it becomes. The stickier the jaggery, the harder the *poka mithoi*. The harder the *poka mithoi*, the tastier it gets. 'I started making the best use of this *pitha*. Whenever I would be late for breakfast, I would pop a few of these and drink some water. When the rice powder in the *pitha* mixes with water, it expands and fills the stomach. Rice is the staple diet of the Assamese people. So here you have another indigenous way to have rice.'

Ingredients

Rice powder	:	6 cups
Jaggery	:	3 cups
Water	:	½ cup
Freshly ground pepper	:	2 tsps

Method

§ Roast the rice powder in small portions in a heavy karai. Stir it continuously. When a sweet smell emanates, remove it from the fire.
§ Mix the freshly ground pepper and the powdered rice.
§ Make a syrup of half of the jaggery and water.
§ Mix a little of the jaggery syrup with a part of rice powder and make firm round balls.
§ Dust the balls with the roasted rice powder.
§ When all the jaggery syrup is used, make some syrup with the other half, mix it with the remaining rice power and make firm round balls as earlier.
§ Serve *poka mithoi* with tea. They can be stored for 2 months.

Note: *Poka mithoi* made with fresh rice powder is often offered to the deity.

Tekeli Pitha
Pitcher Cake (sweet)

Tekeli is a clay pitcher with a long neck. A kettle can also be used to make *tekeli pitha* instead of the clay pitcher. A *tekeli* is used for different purposes in Assamese culture. Starting from the storage of drinking water, rice powder, *pithas* and other eatables, to its use in socio-religious functions. *Doi* (curd) *tekeli* and *gur* (jaggery) *tekeli* are an integral part of any socio-religious function.

Ingredients

New season rice	:	250 gms
Grated coconut	:	100 gms
Sugar	:	30 gms

Method

§ Clean and soak the rice for an hour. Drain well. Pound and sieve.
§ Mix the rice powder with the grated coconut and sugar.
§ Heat water in a kettle or *tekeli*.
§ Fill the cover of the kettle with the rice powder mixture. Take a thin muslin cloth.
§ Invert the cover, holding the muslin cloth so that the rice powder does not fall out.
§ Place the cover over the mouth of the kettle.
§ Steam for 5 minutes or till done.
§ Remove the *tekeli pitha* from the cloth. Serve warm with tea or coffee.
§ *Tekeli pithas* can also be served with sweet chilled milk.

Seventy per cent of the world's Asiatic wild buffaloes are to be found in the Kaziranga National Park.

Tekeli Pitha
Pitcher Cake (savoury)

Tekeli pitha is like a comfort food for me. You can enjoy it with pickle, chutney, any type of meat or simply without any of these. The use of local eggs makes the *tekeli pithas* colourful as the yolks are bright orange in colour. One can also use duck eggs.

Ingredients

New season rice	:	400 gms
Finely chopped onion	:	1 medium-sized
Finely chopped chillies	:	2
Salt	:	to taste
Eggs	:	8
To garnish	:	sliced tomatoes mint leaves

Method

- Clean and soak the rice for an hour. Drain well.
- Pound well and sieve.
- Mix it with a little water to moisten the rice powder.
- Mix the chopped onion, chillies and salt with the powder.
- Heat water in a clay container with a long neck.
- Keep a moist muslin cloth at the mouth of the clay container and make a depression.
- Fill the depression with the rice mixture. Cover it and steam for about 2 minutes.

- Make a depression in the steamed *pitha* and break a raw egg into it.
- Steam for another 3 minutes or till the egg is cooked.
- Remove it carefully from the *tekeli*. Make a few more *tekeli pithas*.
- Decorate *tekeli pithas* with sliced tomatoes and mint leaves and serve them with some pickle and mutton curry.

Note: *Joha* rice is not usually used for making any rice powder. In the villages, a variety of coarse rice is normally used.

Gamosas are offered to elders as a mark of respect specially during Bohag Bihu.

Anguli Pitha
Finger-Like Pithas

Anguli literally means fingers in Assamese and is one of the most relished varieties of *pithas*. Just like fingers, the longer and more slender the *anguli pithas*, the better.

Ingredients

Rice powder	:	150 gms
Salt	:	to taste
Oil	:	4 tbsps
Crushed black pepper	:	½ tsp
Aniseed	:	½ tsp
Water	:	to make the dough
Mustard oil	:	60 ml
Onions (sliced into rings)	:	4 medium-sized
Slit green chillies	:	4
Sliced tomatoes	:	2 medium-sized
Sliced capsicum	:	1 medium-sized
Coconut milk	:	6 tbsps
Grated coconut	:	2 tbsps
Beaten eggs	:	2

Method

§ Make a dough with the rice powder, salt, crushed black pepper, aniseed and water.
§ Make small thin rolls which are about 1½ inch in length.
§ Boil the *pithas* for about 2 minutes in boiling water.

- Dip the *pithas* in cold water and drain well.
- Heat the mustard oil in a karai. Add the sliced onions and green chillies and stir.
- When the onions are soft, add the sliced tomatoes and capsicum. Stir well.
- Add the *aanguli pithas* and sprinkle some salt. Stir gently.
- Add the coconut milk and grated coconut and stir.
- Push the *pithas* away from the centre and pour the beaten eggs. Stir gently.
- Push the *pithas* towards the centre.
- Stir for a minute.
- Serve hot *anguli pithas* with some pickle or sauce.

Aam Aru Bora Chaulor Pitha
Mango and Sticky Rice Pitha

Every special recipe brings back sweet memories. My daughter is very fond of mangoes. Everytime I would make *aam aru bora chaulor pitha* when she was a small kid, she would always ask for more. So mango lovers, if you are in a mood to try out a new mango recipe, try the following one.

Ingredients

Sticky rice	:	400 gms
Jaggery	:	100 gms
Ripe mango pulp	:	4 tbsps
Salt (optional)	:	a pinch
Water	:	to knead the dough
Banana leaves	:	4 medium-sized

Method

- Wash the sticky rice. Soak it for 4-5 hours. Drain well and spread it out to dry.
- Pound the rice.
- Clean and dry the banana leaves. Hold them over a low fire to make them pliable.
- Place the rice powder, jaggery, mango pulp and salt in a bowl and knead to a soft dough by adding water.
- Divide the dough into 4 equal portions and spread it on the banana leaves.
- Fold the leaves and make 4 parcels. Tie each one with a string.

§ Place the parcels, one at a time, over a hot griddle and cook on both sides for about 10 minutes or till done.
§ Let it cool. Unwrap the parcels and serve hot *aam aru bora chaulor pitha* with tea.

Note: Banana or jackfruit pulp can also be used to make this *pitha*. Sugar can also be used instead of jaggery.

Narikolor Laru
Coconut Ladoo

One cannot think of a *Bihu* table spread without *narikolor laru*. The sweetness of the *laru* depends on the freshness of the grated coconut. The sugar just acts as a binding agent. The whiter and rounder the *laru*, the better reflection of the culinary expertise of the housewives of Assam.

Ingredients

Freshly grated coconut	:	4 cups
Sugar	:	2 cups

Method

- Mix the grated coconut with sugar.
- Transfer the coconut and sugar mixture to a karai or pan.
- Cook upon low heat stirring continuously till the mixture turns thick and leaves the sides of the karai or pan.
- When it cools a bit, shape into small round balls of desired size.
- Cool and store in a container.
- Serve *narikolor laru* as a tea-time snack with *pithas*.

The orchid Kapau phul (Rhynchostylis retusa) blooms during spring (Bohag Bihu). This orchid is worn around the hair bun and is an integral part of a Bihu dancer's attire.

Kathali Seppa
Carambola

It is not a *pitha*, but *kathali seppa* is also made during *Bihu*. It is also known as *kordoi* as it resembles the carambola fruit.

Ingredients

Flour	:	150 gms
Ghee	:	35 gms
Warm water	:	to knead the dough
Salt	:	a pinch
Sugar	:	250 gms
Water (for the sugar syrup)	:	200 ml
Cardamom powder	:	1 level tsp
Refined oil	:	for frying

Method

- Mix the flour, ghee and salt together.
- When it resembles bread crumbs, add warm water and make a soft dough. Keep it covered for 10-15 minutes.
- Make 20 balls. Roll out each ball into thin puris.
- Cut into strips with a sharp knife. Do not cut through the ends.
- Hold both the ends and twist them. Press the ends.
- Heat the oil and deep-fry upon medium heat, 2-3 at a time, till light golden brown in colour.
- Keep them on a paper napkin to soak excess oil.
- Boil the sugar and water to make a light syrup.

- Dip the *kathali seppa* into the hot syrup and leave for about 10-12 minutes.
- Remove them from the syrup. Sprinkle cardamom powder and let it cool.
- *Kathali seppa* is a great tea-time snack.

Chaul
Rice

The river Brahmaputra is the lifeline of Assam. *Bura* (old) Luit flows right across the state, making it lush and green. Along the Brahmaputra, you will find on its banks, forest reserves, home to hundreds of varieties of flora and fauna. Animals, especially the rhino are the famous inhabitants of these green valleys. The river has plenty to support its dependents. Human civilisation also thrives on the mighty Brahmaputra.

The Assam valley is in the foothills of the eastern-most range of the Himalayas. Cherrapunji, one of the wettest locations of the world is not very far away from this place. Assam also gets its share of rain. So you have two sources of water. The Brahmaputra keeps the land moist from within the earth and the rain joins in from the skies above. It is in harmony, and almost perfect except in the time of the monsoon rains.

Along the edges of these reserves, you have the cultivation of rice. The people must have settled in these valleys because of the abundance of natural benefits. Basmati rice has its origins along the banks of the Ganges. Along the banks of the Brahmaputra, the *joha* variety of rice is grown which owes its origin to these green valleys. *Joha* rice has a sweet musky aroma which is unique. I remember being told by a shikari of repute, that the aroma of the *joha* rice is so sweet, it attracts big cats like tigers and leopards. He would cook it to attract the cats. There are many stories still going around in the villages, stories of the big cats attacking villages near such reserves, where the sweet smell of *joha* rice lingers. The

Assamese community prefer rice. Though urban people have rice twice daily, the farming communities in the rural areas prefer to have rice thrice a day.

The cultivators normally eat *poita bhat* for breakfast. *Poita bhat* is left-over rice kept soaked in water overnight to ferment. In these valleys, the sun rises at early dawn. The sun is out by 4.30 am. The farmers are out, cultivating their fields when the rest of us are still comfortably tucked in our beds. They normally eat *poita bhat* before they leave for work. The housewives therefore cook some extra *bhat* for dinner. The left-over rice is kept for the men before they leave for work. Necessity is the mother of all inventions. How do you stop the extra rice from going bad, if you don't have a refrigerator? You pour some water over the rice, the cold water stops the rice from drying and from getting spoilt. Left like this overnight, it ferments a little and you get *poita bhat*. It is then eaten with *pura* (roasted) *maach* or potatoes garnished with green chillies, salt and mustard oil. *Poita bhat* keeps the cultivator full and also cool during the hot summer days.

For their midday meal the farmers normally enjoy *komal chaul* or sticky rice in their fields. To make *komal chaul*, the paddy is first soaked overnight. Then it is boiled in plenty of water. The paddy is then drained and dried. Then the chaff is separated from the grain. All this must be completed in the course of a day. The grain known as *komal chaul* gets tender if soaked in water for an hour. *Komal chaul* is a typical Assamese dish eaten with jaggery and curd. Bananas can also be added.

Sticky rice baked in a bamboo hollow (*baanhor chunga*) is a special dish prepared for honoured guests, especially during the *Bihu* festivals.

Rice steamed and wrapped in banana leaves is known as *sewa diya bhat* and it is a typical Assamese rice dish. Sticky rice can also be used for *sewa diya bhat*. *Sewa bhat* is popular among many communities of Assam but more so in Upper Assam.

The people of this land have experimented so much with rice that they have come up with a variety of recipes.

You have *pithas* made out of rice, you have *larus* made out of it, it is consumed simply as it is by boiling it and also eaten for breakfast by fermenting it overnight. So it is not surprising that *laupani*, an indigenous beer is also made by fermenting and maturing rice in pumpkin hollows.

Note: The rice beer made of sticky rice is also called *sanj* and is believed to induce longevity.

Baanhor Chungat Bora Chaul
Sticky Rice in a Bamboo Hollow

The year was 2001. It was the season of *Magh Bihu*. Our Ladies Club took us to an interior village named Lengeri of the Dibrugarh district in Upper Assam as part of the social work it was involved in. Our group was invited for *jalpan* (a light repast) to a local resident's place, where we were served newly harvested sticky rice, curd and jaggery. That has been one of the best *jalpans* of my life and it left all of us asking for more. Out host was generous enough to give all of us some sticky rice baked in bamboo hollows to take home as well.

Ingredients

Sticky rice	:	500 gms
Banana leaves	:	4
Tender bamboo hollows	:	4

Method

§ Clean the rice. Soak it for 5-6 hours.
§ Clean the banana leaves and hold them over a low flame to make them pliable.
§ Drain the rice. Fill the bamboo hollows with the rice leaving a two-inch empty space at the top. Add 4 tbsps of water to each hollow.
§ Seal the bamboo hollows with banana leaves or thatch.
§ Place the bamboo hollows over a slow charcoal fire and rotate them from time to time.

- § When the hollows are evenly heated, remove them from the charcoal fire.
- § Let it cool and split the hollows.
- § Take out the cooked rice which takes the shape of the hollow. Cut into desired size.
- § Serve *baanhor chungat bora chaul* with curd and jaggery.
- § It can also be served with pork, mutton or chicken curry.

Note: To preserve bamboo shoot, boil it in water for 10 minutes. Drain and preserve it in ten per cent brine solution. It should not be exposed to air.

Chunga Chaul
Rice in a Bamboo Hollow

My husband is my inspiration. He appreciates and encourages me when I try innovative recipes. The following one was one of my first variations of rice cooked in bamboo hollows.

Ingredients

Joha rice	:	250 gms
Sticky rice	:	50 gms
Banana leaves	:	2
Chopped onions	:	2 medium-sized
Chopped green chillies	:	2
Finely chopped french beans	:	4
Grated carrot	:	1 medium-sized
Grated ginger	:	1½ tsps
Whole peppers	:	20
Oil	:	1 tbsp
Salt	:	to taste
Tender bamboo hollows	:	2
To garnish	:	1 chilli
		1 tomato
		1 sliced lemon

Method

§ Clean the *joha* and sticky rice. Soak them together for 5-6 hours.
§ Clean the banana leaves and hold them over a low flame to make them pliable.

Jyoti Das

- § Drain the rice. Mix it with the chopped onions, chillies, and beans. Add the grated carrot, ginger, whole peppers, oil and salt as well.
- § Fill the bamboo hollows with the rice mixture leaving a two-inch empty space at the top. Add 3-4 tbsps of water.
- § Seal the hollows with banana leaves.
- § Place the bamboo hollows over gas fire for about 15-20 minutes.
- § Rotate from time to time and let them heat evenly. When done remove from the fire. Let them cool.
- § Split the hollows and take out the rice that takes the shape of the hollow. Cut it into desired size.
- § Garnish with tomatoes, the sliced lemon and the chilli and serve *chunga chaul* on a banana leaf with chicken curry.

Note: Traditionally bamboo hollows are heated directly over a slow charcoal fire. Tender hollows can also be heated in hot ash.

Baanhor Chungat Kharisa Diya Bhat
Fermented Bamboo Shoot Rice in a Bamboo Hollow

Victor Banerjee likes and enjoys Assamese food. He is a moderate eater and usually never takes a second helping. Once when he and his wife Maya came for dinner to our place and I made the following rice dish; he did go for a second helping.

Ingredients

Sticky rice	:	100 gms
Joha rice	:	300 gms
Oil	:	3 tbsps
Finely chopped onions	:	2 medium-sized
Finely chopped chillies	:	2
Kharisa	:	4 tbsps
Soy sauce	:	2 tbsps
Bamboo hollows	:	3
Banana leaves	:	3
Salt	:	to taste

Method

§ Clean and soak the sticky and *joha* rice together for 4-5 hours. Drain out the water.
§ Clean the banana leaves, dry them and hold them over a low flame to make them pliable.
§ Heat the oil in a karai. Add the chopped onions and fry them till soft.

- § Add the chopped green chillies, the rice, *kharisa* and soy sauce and stir fry on medium heat for a minute. Also sprinkle some salt.
- § Fill the bamboo hollows leaving a two-inch empty space at the top. Add 3-4 tbsps of water and seal each hollow with banana leaves.
- § Place the hollows upon low gas fire for 15-20 minutes. First heat the mouth of the hollows. Rotate the hollows from time to time so that the rice cooks evenly.
- § When done, remove from the fire. Split the hollows with a sharp knife.
- § Serve hot *baanhor chungat kharisa diya bhat* with pigeon, pork or duck curry.

Note: Bamboo shoot is an indispensable part of Assamese cuisine. It is an appetite enhancer. It is said to decrease blood pressure and cholesterol. It is also a good source of fibre.

Bor/Pakoras
Fritters

Assam is a haven for different species of flora and fauna. Flowering plants and other vegetation form an integral part of Assamese cuisine.

The flowers and leaves used in cooking often have disease preventing and curing properties. *Bor* which is enjoyed as a side dish or a starter is tasty as well as healthy. Some flowers which have these properties are the *sajina phul* (drumstick flower), *rongalau phul* (pumpkin flower), *bhet phul* (water lily), *aparajeeta* (butterfly pea), *Kanchan* (bauhinia), *bok phul* (Sesbania grandiflora) and so on.

Many such flowers are dried and preserved for later use. The dried flowers of the *tita phul* (Phlogacanthus tubiflorus) and *sewali phul* (Nyctanthes arbortristis) are used to make *bors*, as well as in the preparation of *khar*.

Rongalao Phulor Bor

Pumpkin Flower Fritters

Ingredients

Rongalao phul (pumpkin flowers)	:	8
Rice powder	:	50 gms
Baking soda	:	a pinch
Turmeric powder	:	a pinch
Salt	:	to taste
Water	:	to make the paste
Oil	:	for deep frying

Method

§ Clean and wash the flowers.
§ Make a paste of rice powder, baking soda, turmeric powder, salt and water.
§ Heat the mustard oil in a small karai. Dip the flowers in the rice powder paste.
§ Deep-fry the pumpkin flowers on medium heat, one at a time till crisp and done.
§ Put the fried *bors* on a paper napkin to soak excess oil.
§ Serve hot *rongalao phulor bor* as a snack with tea or as a starter.

Note: Other edible flowers like *bok phul* (Sesbania grandiflora) is also enjoyed as fritters. For taste and flavour, fennel, *ajowan* or nigella can be added. *Bok phul* which is rich in vitamin A is also a laxative. It is also good for colds, headaches, cough and the memory and works as an appetiser as well.

Sewali Phulor Bor
Coral Jasmine Pakoras

Ingredients

Fresh *sewali phul* (Coral Jasmine)	:	2 tbsps
Besan/gram flour	:	5 tbsps
Baking soda	:	a pinch
Turmeric powder	:	a pinch
Salt	:	to taste
Water	:	to make the batter
Nigella	:	a pinch
Oil	:	for deep frying

Method

§ Clean and soak the flowers in water for a minute and squeeze out the water.
§ Make a thick batter of *besan*, baking soda, turmeric powder, salt and water. Also add nigella and the flowers.
§ Heat oil in a small karai. Deep-fry the *bors* by dropping dollops of the batter in hot mustard oil on medium heat till golden brown.
§ Soak excess oil on a paper napkin.
§ Serve hot *sewali phulor bors* with chutney as a starter.
§ The *bors* will have a slight bitter taste.

Note: The tender leaves and flowers of the drumstick tree (Moringa oleifera), *tita phul* (Phlogacanthus tubiflorus) and the tender leaves of *sewali phul* can also be made into *bors*.

Mosmosiya Bengena Bhoja
Crunchy Brinjal Fritters

Ingredients

Bengena (brinjal)	:	1 (150 gms)
Salt	:	to taste
Besan	:	3 tbsps
Rice powder	:	3 tbsps
Baking powder	:	a pinch
Turmeric powder	:	a pinch
Chilli powder	:	½ level tsp
Oil	:	for deep frying
Water	:	to make the batter

Method

§ Clean the *bengena* and cut it into thin round slices or long pieces.
§ Make a batter of besan, rice powder, baking powder, turmeric powder, chilli powder, salt and water. Keep it covered for 15 minutes.
§ Heat the mustard oil in a small karai. Dip a thin *bengena* piece in the batter and deep fry on medium heat.
§ Turn occasionally till it turns golden in colour and becomes crisp. Drain on an absorbent paper.
§ Enjoy m*osmosiya bengena bhoja* with rice and daal.

Note: Crispy *bengena bhoja* is normally served in Assamese feasts. White pumpkin, *potol* (Trichosanthes diocia), pumpkin and bottlegourd are also similarly fried.

Maachor Konir Bor
Fish Egg Pakoras

Ingredients

Fish egg	:	250 gms
Rice powder	:	2 tbsps
Chopped green chillies	:	2
Finely chopped onion	:	1 medium-sized
Grated ginger	:	1 tsp
Turmeric powder	:	a pinch
Salt	:	to taste
Mustard oil	:	for frying
To garnish	:	sliced onions

Method

§ Clean the fish eggs in water and drain.
§ Remove the transparent sheet or coating around the fish roe cluster.
§ Add the rice powder, chopped green chillies, the finely chopped onion and grated ginger to the eggs.
§ Also sprinkle the turmeric powder and salt to taste. Mix well with your hands.
§ Heat the mustard oil in a small karai and deep-fry the pakoras on medium heat till golden brown.
§ Garnish with sliced onions.
§ Serve *maachor konir bor* as a second course with *paro manxor jhul*.
§ They can also be served as a starter with chutney.

Variation: Roast the fish eggs by wrapping them in a banana leaf. Add fresh mustard oil, finely chopped onions, chillies, coriander and salt to the cooked fish eggs. Mash and serve as a side dish.

Note: Fish egg pakoras are also enjoyed as *tenga* or as a curry.

Masur Dailor Bor
Red Lentil Pakoras

Ingredients

Red lentil/*masoor dail*	:	100 gms
Rice	:	25 gms
Chopped coriander leaves	:	1 tbsp
Chopped onions	:	2 medium-sized
Chopped green chillies	:	2
Cumin seeds	:	a pinch
Salt	:	to taste
Mustard oil	:	for frying

Method

§ Clean, wash and soak the lentil and the rice for three hours.
§ Grind the lentil and rice together to a smooth paste.
§ Add the chopped coriander leaves, chopped onions, chopped green chillies and cumin seeds to the lentil paste.
§ Sprinkle salt and mix well.
§ Heat the mustard oil in a small karai. Fry the pakoras on a medium flame till crisp.
§ Keep them on a paper napkin to soak excess oil.
§ Serve *masur dailor bor* as a starter or with rice and daal.

Note: Adding some rice while making the paste makes the *bor* crisp.
Broken moong daal is also used to make pakoras.
Tender spinach (whole) are dipped in rice powder batter, fried in mustard oil and served as *paleng pat bhoja*.

Khar
Alkali

In my early childhood I have seen our gardener chop down *aatheya* (a species of banana: Musa sapientum), under the supervision of my father. Very meticulously, the roots would be dug out. Then the trunk along with the roots would be cut into small pieces. I would intently watch this yearly ritual, religiously carried out between October to mid November. This is part of the initial stages of the preparation of the Assamese *khar*.

Khar is inseparable from Assamese cuisine. It is so much a part of the Assamese culture that the people of this land are often called *khar khua Asomiya*.

Khar is the first course of an Assamese midday meal. It is consumed only during the day and it is often limited to once a week. An old grandmother's tale has it that there are immense benefits from having *khar*. It cleans one's system and detoxifies the body. It clears the throat to such an extent that often vocal performers with a sore throat go on a diet of steaming hot *khar bhat* (rice) with mustard oil and salt.

An Assamese woman's culinary dexterity is judged by how well she can make *khar* and also upon the varieties of *khar* she can make. Though papaya *khar* is the most common and popular, it can be made from any vegetable and herb. My hot favourite is the one which is made with the head of a fish.

Khar also known as *kolakhar* in Assam is an indigenous soda made at home. It is made by burning the dried trunk or roots of chopped *aatheya*. Firstly, the pieces are left in the open to dry and when night falls, the dew is allowed to settle on it. It is believed that the dew on the pieces accentuates the taste of the final product. This process is carried on till the pieces are completely dry. Then the dried pieces are burnt and are again left outside for the dew to settle in. The ashes are then stored in an air-tight container (in rural areas the common practice is to store it in an earthen pot) and *kolakhar* is ready for use. When required, the ashes are mixed with water and then filtered. The alkaline liquid is golden in colour.

Khar can also be made with the peel of the above mentioned *aatheya*. First the peel of the banana should be dried. Then it is burnt and the burnt peel is immediately dipped in water. The water changes to a golden colour. It is filtered and can be stored in a bottle.

It is worth mentioning that the *khar* made from the roots or banana peel is stronger than the *khar* made of the dried trunk. A little sugar can be used while making *khar*. Fresh mustard oil is always added just before it is served for an authentic flavour.

Note: If you are unable to find *kolakhar* you can use sodium bicarbonate as a substitute.

Amitar Khar
Papaya Khar

Ingredients

Papaya (cleaned and diced)	:	500 gms
Mustard oil	:	2 tbsps
Fenugreek seeds	:	a pinch
Garlic cloves	:	6
Fresh chillies	:	2
Salt	:	to taste
Sugar	:	a pinch
Kolakhar (Indigenous soda)	:	1 tbsp
Hot water	:	100 ml
Ginger paste	:	2 tsps
Mustard oil	:	1 tbsp
To garnish	:	fresh tender mint leaves
	:	fresh red chillies

Method

§ Heat the oil in a wok. Add the fenugreek seeds. When they turn black, remove them from the oil.
§ Add the garlic, papaya and green chillies. Sprinkle salt and sugar. Stir well for about half a minute.
§ Reduce the heat. Cover and cook. Stir occasionally.
§ After 6-7 minutes, remove the cover. Add the *kolakhar*. Stir and cover for 2 minutes.
§ Add the water. Cover and let it simmer. Add the ginger.

- § When the papaya is soft, remove from the fire.
- § Garnish with mint leaves and fresh red chillies.
- § Add the mustard oil just before serving it.
- § Enjoy *amitar khar* with steaming hot *joha* rice as a first course for lunch.

Note: *Khar* can be similarly made with bottlegourd and cucumber.

Sanmehali Kharor Lagot Kathal Guti
Mixed Khar with Jackfruit Seeds

Ingredients

Jackfruit seeds	:	20
Mustard oil	:	2 tbsps
Garlic cloves	:	12
Papaya (diced)	:	250 gms
Bottlegourd (diced)	:	250 gms
Cucumber (diced)	:	250 gms
Fresh green chillies	:	2
Salt and sugar	:	to taste
Kolakhar (Indigenous soda)	:	1½ tbsps
Hot water	:	50 ml
Crushed ginger	:	1 tbsp
Mustard oil	:	1 tbsp
To garnish	:	green chillies

Method

§ Remove the outer dry skin of the jackfruit seeds.
§ Soak the seeds in water for half an hour and remove the reddish inner skin with a sharp knife.
§ Heat the oil in a wok or karai. Sauté the garlic and add the diced vegetables, jackfruit seeds and chillies.
§ Sprinkle salt and sugar. Reduce the heat and cover. Stir occasionally.
§ After 5 minutes, add the *kolakhar*. Stir and cover for 5 minutes.

- § Add the water. Let it simmer till done. Add the crushed ginger and remove from the fire.
- § Add the fresh mustard oil and garnish it with green chillies.
- § Serve rice and *sanmehali kharor logot kathal goti* as a first course for lunch.

Note: If unavailable, one can use ¼ level tsp of sodium bicarbonate instead of *kolakhar*.

Mati Dailor Khar
Black Gram Khar

Ingredients

Black gram (without skin)	:	150 gms
Water	:	750 ml
Mustard oil	:	2 tbsps
Fenugreek seeds	:	a pinch
Dry red chillies	:	2
Chopped garlic	:	2 tbsps
Kolakhar (Indigenous soda)	:	1½ tbsps
Ginger paste	:	1 tbsp
Salt and sugar	:	to taste
Mustard oil	:	1 tbsp
To garnish	:	green chillies – 4

Method

§ Clean and soak the black gram overnight. Boil the black gram in a pressure cooker in 750 ml of plain water.
§ Heat the oil in a wok or karai. Add the fenugreek seeds. When the seeds turn red, add the dry chillies and chopped garlic.
§ Stir fry. When the garlic turns brown, add the hot boiled black gram, *kolakhar*, ginger paste, salt and sugar. Cover.
§ When the gravy thickens, remove the *mati dailor khar* from the fire.
§ Add the mustard oil to enhance the flavour of the *khar*.
§ Garnish with green chillies and serve hot with rice.

Note: Turmeric powder is not used while making any type of *khar*.

Masur Dail Aru Baahgajor Khar
Red Lentil and Bamboo Shoot Khar

Ingredients

Red lentil	:	150 gms
Water	:	1 litre
Freshly diced bamboo shoot	:	150 gms
Kolakhar (Indigenous soda)	:	1½ tbsps
Mustard oil	:	3 tbsps
Mustard seeds	:	½ level tsp
Dry red chillies	:	3
Chopped garlic	:	1 tbsp
Ginger paste	:	1 tbsp
Salt and sugar	:	to taste
To garnish	:	mustard oil – 2 tbsps

Method

§ Clean, wash and soak the red lentil for three hours.
§ Pressure cook in 750 ml of water.
§ In 250 ml of boiling water, boil the bamboo shoot for about 5 minutes. Also add the salt and the *kolakhar*. Drain well.
§ Heat the mustard oil. Splutter the mustard seeds in it. Add broken red chillies and chopped garlic.
§ When the garlic is almost brown, add the boiled bamboo shoot. Stir for a minute.

§ Add the hot lentil, salt and sugar. When the gravy thickens, add the ginger paste. Stir well.
§ Garnish with mustard oil and serve *masur dail aru baanhgajor khar* with sticky rice baked in bamboo hollows or *sewa diya bhat*.

Bamboo is an integral part of the economic, cultural and social fabric of Assam. There are about twenty-nine types of bamboo found in Assam.

Sajina Pator Khar

Drumstick Leaves Khar

Ingredients

Red lentil	:	100 gms
Drumstick tender leaves	:	40 gms
Mustard oil	:	3 tbsps
Dry red chillies	:	2
Garlic cloves	:	5
Salt and sugar	:	to taste
Kolakhar (Indigenous soda)	:	1 ½ tbsps
Finely chopped ginger	:	½ tbsp
Hot water	:	500 ml
Mustard oil	:	1 tbsp
To garnish	:	green chillies – 4

Method

§ Clean the lentil and soak for half an hour. Also clean the drumstick leaves.
§ Heat oil in a pressure cooker. Add the red chillies and garlic cloves. Stir.
§ When the garlic changes colour, add the lentil and drumstick leaves. Stir for a minute.
§ Add salt, sugar, *kolakhar* and ginger. Stir well.
§ Add water and bring the pressure cooker to full pressure.
§ Reduce the heat to minimum and cook for two minutes. When it cools, open the pressure cooker. Stir well.

§ Add mustard oil to enhance the flavour. Garnish with green chillies.
§ Serve *sajina pator khar* as a first course with rice.

Sajinar Khar
Drumstick Khar

Ingredients

Drumsticks (tender)	:	300 gms
Red lentil	:	2 tbsps
Mustard oil	:	3 tbsps
Fenugreek seeds	:	a pinch
Fresh green chillies	:	2
Crushed garlic	:	1 tbsp
Salt and sugar	:	to taste
Kolakhar (Indigenous soda)	:	1 tbsp
Chopped ginger	:	2 tsps
Warm water	:	300 ml
Mustard oil	:	2 tbsps
To garnish	:	green chillies – 6

Method

- Cut the drumsticks into pieces, each 1½ inch in length. Soak the lentil for half an hour.
- Heat the oil in a pressure cooker. Add the fenugreek seeds, chillies and crushed garlic. Stir for a few seconds.
- Add the drumsticks and the lentil. Fry for a minute on medium heat.
- Add salt, sugar, *kolakhar* and the chopped ginger. Stir well.
- Add warm water and bring the cooker to full pressure. Reduce the heat to minimum and cook for 3 more minutes.

§ When it cools, open the cover. Add mustard oil for flavour and garnish with green chillies.
§ Serve *sajinar khar* with rice as a first course for lunch with *sewa diya bhat*.

Note: If you have run out of your shampoo, try using *kolakhar* instead.

Posolar Khar
Banana Stem Khar

Ingredients

Tender banana stems	:	500 gms
Salt	:	½ tsp
Red lentil	:	70 gms
Mustard oil	:	3 tbsps
Fenugreek seeds	:	a pinch
Dry red chillies	:	2
Chopped onions	:	2 medium-sized
Garlic paste	:	1 tbsp
Ginger paste	:	1 tbsp
Green chillies	:	2
Salt and sugar	:	to taste
Kolakhar (Indigenous soda)	:	1½ tbsps
Warm water	:	500 ml
Mustard oil	:	2 tbsps
To garnish	:	mint leaves green chillies – 1 red capsicum – 4 pieces

Method

- § Remove the outer layer of the banana stem. Take the soft and tender stem. Clean it and chop finely.
- § Add salt to it and crush the chopped stem with the fingertips. Do not wash the stem after chopping it.
- § Clean and soak the lentil for half an hour.

- § Heat the oil in a pressure cooker. Add the fenugreek seeds and dry red chillies. Remove the seeds when they turn black.
- § Add the chopped onions and stir till the onions are soft but not brown.
- § Add the ginger and garlic paste. Fry for a minute. Add the green chillies.
- § Add the chopped banana stem, red lentil, salt, sugar and *kolakhar*. Stir upon a low flame for 2 minutes.
- § Add water. Close the pressure cooker. Increase the heat. Bring the cooker to full pressure. Reduce the heat and keep on the fire for 4-5 minutes.
- § When slightly cool, open the cover. Add the mustard oil.
- § Close the cooker and open it after two minutes.
- § Serve hot *posolar khar* and garnish it with mint leaves, sliced capsicum and green chilli. Relish it with sticky rice baked in a bamboo hollow and chopped ginger.

Note: The tender stem of any type of banana can also be used to make the above dish. In Assam, we use the stem of *aatheya* for its medical properties.

The dressed sprout of the banana tree is tastier. One can add a fish head to this recipe as well.

It is taken as a remedy for flatulence. Tuberculosis patients are continuously given the *posola* of *aatheya* for 8-10 days.

Xaakor Khar
Herbs Khar

Ingredients

Mustard leaves *(xarioh xaak)*	:	75 gms
Spinach *(paleng xaak)*	:	75 gms
Fenugreek leaves *(methi xaak)*	:	50 gms
Indian pennywort *(bor manimoni)*	:	50 gms
Mustard oil	:	3 tbsps
Fenugreek seeds	:	a pinch
Crushed garlic	:	2 tbsps
Green chillies	:	2
Kolakhar (Indigenous soda)	:	1 tbsp
Salt and sugar	:	to taste
Mustard seed paste	:	2 tbsps
Black pepper paste	:	1 tsp
To garnish	:	mustard oil – 2 tsps

Method

§ Clean and chop the *xaak*.
§ Heat mustard oil in a wok or pan. Splutter the fenugreek seeds.
§ Add the crushed garlic and chillies. Stir. When it changes colour, add the chopped *xaak*.
§ Fry for 2 minutes. Add *kolakhar,* salt and sugar. Stir occasionally.
§ Reduce heat. Add the mustard paste and pepper paste. Stir well.
§ When done, add the mustard oil.
§ Serve *xaakor khar* as a first course of lunch with plain rice.

Note: *Xaak* is a plant without any woody stem.

Indian Pennywort whose scientific name is centella asiatica is used for curing schizophrenia, hysteria and spasmodic respiratory disorders. Chewing of 4 fresh leaves on an empty stomach enhances memory. Chewing of 10 fresh leaves also purifies blood. It also kills worms, controls blood pressure and is good for stomach disorders. Known as the king of herbs, its curry is made with or without fish for its medicinal properties.

Chutney

Chutneys are always welcome in any season. Medicinal herbs and mustard seeds are used to make delicious chutneys. During hot summer days, the taste of chutneys like *pani tenga* with plain rice and daal is out of this world. For any stomach related problems, you can have chutneys of amla, Indian pennywort, *mosundari* (Houttuynia cordata) etc. Chutneys made of coriander leaves, mint leaves and curry leaves are popular. If a chutney made with a certain herb is to be eaten for its medicinal properties, garlic and salt are the only other ingredients added to it.

Kharoli
Fermented Mustard Powder with Alkali

Ingredients

Black mustard seeds	:	150 gms
Lai seeds (optional)	:	25 gms
Salt	:	to taste
Chilli powder	:	1 tsp
Kolakhar(Indigenous soda)	:	to knead with the ground seeds
Banana leaf	:	1

Method

§ Clean and wash the seeds and dry them in the sun.
§ Clean the banana leaf and hold it over a fire to make it pliable.
§ Grind the dried seeds and sieve.
§ On the wrong side of the banana leaf put the ground powder. Add the salt and the chilli powder and knead, adding a litttle *kolakhar* at a time.
§ Knead well for 10 minutes or until the oil appears on the leaf.
§ Make a ball, flatten it and wrap it to form a parcel. Tie the parcel with a string.
§ Keep the parcel inside a container and keep it in a warm place.
§ After three days, the *kharoli* is ready to eat as a chutney.

Note: *Lai* is a variety of spinach whose scientific name is Brassica rugosa.

Pani Tenga
Fermented Mustard Powder with a Souring Agent

Ingredients

Mustard seeds	:	150 gms
Lai seeds (optional)	:	25 gms
Thekera (cocum)	:	15 gms
Banana leaf	:	1
Salt and sugar	:	to taste
Chilli powder	:	1 tsp

Method

- Clean, wash and dry the seeds. Grind the dried seeds together and sieve.
- Soak the *thekera* in a little water for an hour. Mash it and strain the water.
- Clean the banana leaf. Dry it and soften it upon a fire.
- On the wrong side of the banana leaf, put the dry ground powder. Add the salt, sugar and the chilli powder.
- Add the *thekera* juice, a little at a time, to the powder and knead it with the fingertips for about 10 minutes or until the oil seeps from the dough.
- Make a ball. Flatten it and wrap it with the banana leaf like a parcel.
- Tie the parcel and keep it inside a container. Keep the container in a warm place.
- On the third day, the *pani tenga* is ready to eat.

Note: The juice of any citric fruit can be used to make *pani tenga*.

Kharisa
Fermented Bamboo Shoot

Ingredients

Young and tender bamboo shoot	:	2
Green chillies	:	10

Method

§ Peel the bamboo shoot and clean it thoroughly. Drain the water.
§ Grate the bamboo shoot.
§ Store it in dry glass bottles with the fresh chillies.
§ After two weeks, the *kharisa* will become sour and ready for use.

Note: Dry *kharisa* is also a delicacy. It can be used to flavour fried chicken, pork and vegetables. Cat fish fried with dry *kharisa* is used as a medicine and given to patients recovering from chicken pox.

Kharisar Chutney

Take 2-3 tbsps of fermented bamboo shoot or *kharisa*. Add some mustard oil, chopped fresh green or red chillies and salt in a bowl and mix well. Serve as a chutney with rice.

Note: It can be use to garnish fried potatoes and fried chicken.

Kesa Amar Chutney
Raw Mango Chutney

Ingredients

Raw mangoes	:	2
Mint leaves	:	a few
Chopped green chillies	:	2-3
Red chilli powder	:	a pinch
Sugar	:	2 tsps
Salt	:	according to taste
Mustard oil	:	2 tsps

Method

- Take two firm raw mangoes. Clean and peel the mangoes and grate them.
- Clean the mint leaves and tear them with the hands.
- Mix the grated mangoes, chopped green chillies, mint leaves and chilli powder in a bowl.
- Also add the sugar, the salt and the mustard oil. Mix well.
- Serve *kesa amar chutney* in a small bowl.

There are about a thousand varieties of mangoes in India.

Podinar Chutney
Mint Chutney

Ingredients

Mint leaves	:	1 bunch
Raw mango	:	½
Green chillies	:	4
Garlic cloves	:	12
Salt	:	to taste
Sugar	:	to taste

Method

- Clean the mint leaves.
- Peel an unripe mango, take half of it and cut it into pieces.
- Grind the mango pieces, mint leaves, green chillies and garlic cloves together to a smooth paste.
- Add salt and sugar.
- *Podinar chutney* is best served chilled.

Note: Instead of raw mangoes, lemon juice, tamarind, cocum, olives or amla can be used.

Konbilahir Chutney
Cherry Tomato Chutney

Ingredients

Cherry tomatoes	:	100 gms
Coriander leaves	:	a small bunch
Garlic cloves	:	20
Green chillies	:	2-3
Lemon *(kaji nemu)* juice	:	1½ tbsps
Salt	:	to taste
Sugar	:	to taste

Method

- Clean the tomatoes.
- Remove the seeds of the tomatoes.
- Grind the tomatoes, coriander leaves, garlic cloves and green chillies to a coarse paste.
- Add the lemon juice, salt and sugar.
- Mix well and serve in a small bowl.
- *Konbilahir chutney* and plain rice is a great combination. Add a few drops of fresh mustard oil before serving it.
- It can also be served with hot parathas.

Note: The scientific name of *kaji nemu* (lemon) is Citrus acida. Its juice is a cure for some eye diseases.

Amlokhir Chutney
Amla (Indian Gooseberry) Chutney

Ingredients

Dry *thekera* (cocum) pieces	:	3
Green chillies	:	3
Amlokhi (amla/Indian gooseberry)	:	12
Coriander leaves	:	1 small bunch
Garlic cloves	:	10
Salt	:	to taste
Sugar	:	to taste

Method

§ Clean the *thekera* in one tablespoon of water.
§ Slit the green chillies and remove the seeds.
§ Grind the *amlokhi*, coriander leaves, *thekera*, green chillies and garlic cloves together to a smooth paste.
§ Add salt and sugar to taste.
§ Serve *amlokhir chutney* in a small bowl.

Note: Amla chutney made without chillies controls asthma and cures stomach problems. *Amlokhi* controls cancer, gives energy and removes fat. It can also control ageing because of the presence of folic acid which has antioxidant properties.

Dail
Lentil

In Assamese cuisine, every meal normally includes lentil or *dail*. In the villages, the most popular lentil is black gram. Black gram is known as *mati dail* in Assam. It is prepared with indigenous soda (*kolakhar*), duck meat, tomatoes, bamboo shoot, elephant apple etc. Split moong *dail* is eaten after breaking a fast and is made with vegetables. It is not tempered in hot oil and instead, crushed ginger and pure ghee is added towards the end of cooking. Red lentil is relished with herbs or tomatoes. Yellow gram is a favourite dish with plain rice, mashed eggs and potatoes. Bengal gram is best enjoyed with mixed vegetables (*labra bhaji*) and parathas.

Aada Diya Mogur Dail
Moong Daal with Crushed Ginger

Ingredients

Moong daal	:	100 gms
Water	:	500 ml
Salt	:	to taste
Sugar	:	a pinch
Ginger (crushed)	:	1 inch piece
Pure ghee	:	1 tbsp

Method

§ Clean, wash and soak the daal for an hour.
§ Put the daal in a pressure cooker and add water, salt and sugar.
§ Close the cooker and bring it to full pressure.
§ Reduce the heat to minimum and keep upon the fire for a minute. Let it cool.
§ Open the cooker and add the crushed ginger and pure ghee. Stir well and keep it covered for a minute.
§ Serve hot *ada diya mogur dail* with rice as a first course for dinner.

Note: In Assamese, *maah* is the generic name for all types of pulses and beans.

Fola Mogur Dail
Split Green Gram with the Skin

Ingredients

Split green gram (with the skin)	:	200 gms
Brinjal	:	70 gms
Unripe papaya	:	100 gms
Potatoes	:	2 medium-sized
Water	:	600 ml
Ginger juice	:	2 tbsps
Pure ghee	:	1 tbsp
Salt	:	to taste

Method

§ Soak the split green gram for 4 hours. Wash the green gram. Remove only half of the skins while washing.
§ Peel the brinjal, papaya and potatoes and cut into pieces of the desired size.
§ In a pressure cooker, put the green gram, vegetables, water and salt. Close the pressure cooker.
§ Bring the cooker to full pressure. Reduce the heat to minimum and keep upon the fire for five minutes.
§ When it cools, open the cover.
§ Add the ginger juice and pure ghee. Stir well and cover for a minute.
§ Serve *fola mogur dail* with plain rice or hot chapattis.

Masur Dailot Outenga
Red Lentil with Elephant Apple

Ingredients

Red lentil	:	100 gms
Poka outenga(Ripe elephant apple)	:	½
Water	:	150 ml + 600 ml
Turmeric powder	:	½ tsp
Mustard oil	:	3 tbsps
Mustard seeds	:	½ tsp
Chopped tomatoes	:	250 gms
Green chillies	:	3
Salt and sugar	:	to taste
To garnish	:	Few sprigs of coriander leaves

Method

§ Clean and soak the lentil for half an hour.
§ Remove the outer thick coating and inner core of the *outenga*. Cut the middle layer of the *outenga* into one inch pieces.
§ Wash the *outenga* pieces. Pound the pieces to make them soft and pressure cook in 150 ml of water.
§ Boil the lentil adding 600 ml of water and turmeric powder in a pressure cooker.
§ Heat the mustard oil in a karai. Splutter the mustard seeds in the oil and add the tomatoes.

Jyoti Das

§ When the tomatoes are soft, add the hot red lentil, *outenga* with its juice, green chillies, salt and sugar.
§ Cover and cook for 2 minutes. Remove from the fire.
§ Serve hot *masur dailot outenga* with plain rice, garnished with coriander leaves and a fresh green chilli.

Note: It can be strained and had as a soup. In place of ripe elephant apples, one can add olives, hog-plums (*aomora*) and Chinese date plums (*bogori*).

These are plenty of *outenga* trees in the forests of Assam. Wild elephants enjoy eating *outenga*, and hence the name elephant apple.

Mati Dailor Lagot Outenga
Black Gram with Elephant Apple

Ingredients

Split black gram	:	150 gms
Outenga (Elephant apple)	:	½
Mustard oil	:	2 tbsps
Mustard seeds	:	½ level tsp
Red dry chillies	:	2
Turmeric powder	:	½ tsp
Salt and sugar	:	to taste
Warm water	:	800 ml
To garnish	:	Few sprigs of coriander leaves

Method

§ Soak the black gram overnight. Wash and clean the black gram.
§ Remove the outer thick coating and inner core of the *outenga*. Make small pieces of the middle layer and pound it till soft.
§ Heat the oil in a pressure cooker. Splutter the mustard seeds in it and add broken red dry chillies. Stir well.
§ Add the *outenga* and stir fry upon medium heat for about a minute.
§ Add the black gram, turmeric powder and salt. Stir fry for another minute.
§ Add sugar and water. Close the pressure cooker. Bring the cooker to full pressure. Reduce the heat to minimum and keep upon the fire for about 10 minutes.

- § Remove the cooker from the fire. Cool. Open the pressure cooker and garnish the dish with coriander leaves.
- § Serve *mati dailor lagot outenga* with plain rice and fresh green chillies.

Butor Dailor Lagot Kharisa
Bengal Gram with Fermented Bamboo Shoot

Ingredients

Bengal gram	: 200 gms
Kharisa (fermented bamboo shoot)	: 3 tbsps
Warm water	: 800 ml
Turmeric powder	: ½ tsp
Mustard oil	: 2 tbsps
Dry red chillies	: 2
Fenugreek seeds	: a pinch
Salt and sugar	: according to taste

Method

§ Clean the Bengal gram and soak for half an hour.
§ Pressure cook the gram with salt, turmeric powder and water.
§ Heat the mustard oil in a karai. Add dry red chillies and fenugreek seeds.
§ When the seeds turn red, add the *kharisa*. Stir for half a minute.
§ Add the boiled Bengal gram and let it cook for 5 minutes.
§ Serve it hot. *Butor dailor lagot kharisa* goes well with parathas.

Note: Instead of *kharisa*, freshly sliced bamboo shoot can also be added.

Arahor Dailor Lagot Sajina Pat

Yellow Gram with Drumstick Leaves

Ingredients

Yellow gram	:	200 gms
Drumstick leaves	:	70 gms
Hot water	:	800 ml
Turmeric powder	:	½ tsp
Salt and sugar	:	to taste
Oil	:	3 tbsps
Bay leaves	:	2
Green cardamom	:	4
Dry red chillies	:	2
Asafoetida (hing)	:	a pinch
Chopped onions	:	2 medium-sized
Pure ghee	:	1 level tsp

Method

§ Clean and soak the daal for an hour.
§ Clean and wash the drumstick leaves.
§ Pressure cook the daal with water, turmeric powder and salt till tender.
§ Heat the oil. Add the bay leaves, cardamom, chillies, hing and onions, one by one, and stir till the onions are soft.

- § Add the drumstick leaves and stir fry upon medium heat for a minute.
- § Add the hot daal and cook till the daal thickens.
- § Remove from the fire. Add pure ghee.
- § Serve *arahor dailor lagot sajina pat* with rice or chappatis.

Note: Drumstick leaves are known to be a good cure for high blood pressure, heart problems and fever. It prevents skin diseases and is also good for toothaches and nervous debility.

Moringa oleifera (drumstick) has its origin in Tamil Nadu. It grows mainly in subtropical and semi-arid tropical regions.

Maachar Muri Ghonto
Fish Head with Moong Daal

Ingredients

Rohu fish head	:	750 gms (make 4 pieces)
Salt	:	1 level tsp
Turmeric powder	:	½ tsp
Oil	:	for frying the fish head pieces
Moong daal	:	200 gms
Mustard oil	:	3 tbsps
Cumin seeds	:	½ level tsp
Dry red chillies	:	2
Chopped onions	:	2 medium-sized
Bay leaves	:	3
Cumin seed paste	:	1 tsp
Garlic paste	:	1 tsp
Ginger paste	:	1 tsp
Salt	:	to taste
Turmeric powder	:	1 tsp
Hot water	:	800 ml
Green cardamom (crushed)	:	4
Cinnamon (crushed)	:	1 (1 inch stick)
Pure ghee	:	1 tsp

Method

§ Clean the fish head pieces.

- § Sprinkle salt and turmeric powder and rub well.
- § Heat the mustard oil and fry the fish pieces till half done.
- § Roast the moong daal till slightly red. Wash and drain.
- § Heat fresh mustard oil in a pressure cooker. Add cumin seeds and chillies. When the seeds turn red, add the onions and the bay leaves.
- § Fry upon medium heat till the onions are soft. Add the cumin seed paste, garlic paste and ginger paste. Stir well.
- § Sprinkle water a couple of times while frying. When the oil separates from the masala, add the fish head pieces and the daal. Sprinkle salt and turmeric powder.
- § Stir for a minute. Add water and the crushed cardamom and cinnamon.
- § Close the cooker. Bring it to full pressure.
- § Reduce the heat to minimum. Keep it upon the fire for 6-7 minutes and remove the cooker from the fire. Let it cool and then open the cooker. Add pure ghee and mix well.
- § Serve *maachar muri ghonto* as a second course with rice after *khar*.

Vegetables

Assamese people eat lots of vegetables. Herbs are always a part of the midday meal. A typical Assamese meal consists of 2-3 vegetable dishes and a chutney.

Except for some special dishes, most of the vegetables are made without spices. Baked or steamed vegetables are relished with fresh green chillies, coriander leaves and fresh mustard oil. While making *xaak* (herbs), garlic is usually used if they are eaten for their medicinal values. Vegetables are allowed to cook in their own juices on low heat to get the natural flavours and tastes.

In Assam, there are about three thousand species of plants which have medicinal properties and the people of Assam take advantage of nature's bounty.

Herbs are picked before sunrise. From ancient times, it is a belief of the elderly village people that the actual fragrance of the *xaak* evaporates when the sun rises. *Xaak* is also very fresh before sunrise. That is why it is a common sight, specially in the rural areas to see old women chewing *tamul* (betel nut) and *paan* enter their kitchen garden before sunrise with a *kharahi* (bamboo basket) to collect *xaak*. This is something I had been seeing since my childhood. The constant chewing of *tamul paan* exercise the jaws and keep the faces of these women wrinkle-free.

The addition of fresh *xaak* like coriander in a salad, baked dish, pulses and a sour curry (*tenga*) transforms the taste of the food and makes it appetising.

The addition of certain varieties of *xaak* to certain vegetables or curries makes a dish sumptuous and healthy. For example, red lentil with *khutura xaak* (green calalu), catfish with king tonic, drumstick leaves with yellow gram, fenugreek leaves with potatoes and many others, are great combinations.

Dhekia Patot Diya
Dhekia Baked in a Banana Leaf

Ingredients

Dhekia xaak	:	200 gms
Poppy seeds	:	100 gms
Chopped green chillies	:	1 tsp
Grated ginger	:	1 level tsp
Mustard oil	:	1 tbsp (to bake) + 2 tbsps
Banana leaf	:	1
Salt	:	to taste

Method

§ Clean the *xaak*. Chop it coarsely.
§ Make a fine paste of the poppy seeds.
§ Mix the *xaak*, poppy seed paste, chillies, ginger and 1 tbsp of mustard oil.
§ Clean the banana leaf, dry it and pass it over a low fire to make it pliable.
§ Put the *xaak* on the banana leaf and wrap it like a parcel. Tie it with a string.
§ Place the parcel on a grill over a moderate flame. Roast both sides till done.
§ Open the parcel. Add the salt and 2 tbsps of mustard oil and mix it well.
§ Serve hot or cold *dhekia patot diya* with rice.

Note: One can use mustard seeds instead of poppy seeds. The quantity of mustard seeds should be 25 gms.

The scientific name of *dhekia xaak* is Diplazium esculentum.

Khutura Bhaji
Fried Green Calalu

Ingredients

Khutura xaak	:	250 gms
Brinjal	:	150 gms
Mustard oil	:	3 tbsps
Fenugreek seeds	:	a pinch
Sliced onion	:	1 medium-sized
Sliced garlic	:	1 tsp
Green chilli	:	1
Turmeric powder	:	½ level tsp
Salt	:	to taste

Method

§ Clean and chop the *xaak*. Cut the brinjal into pieces of desired size.
§ Heat the oil in a karai. Add the fenugreek seeds.
§ When the seeds are red, add the onion and garlic. Stir well.
§ When the onions are slightly brown, add the *xaak*, green chilli, brinjal and turmeric powder.
§ Stir fry upon medium heat for a while. Add the salt and cover.
§ Stir occasionally. When done, remove from the fire.
§ Serve *khutura bhaji* as a first course with plain rice.

Note: *Khutura* is a *xaak* of the Amaranthus species. Brinjal with *khutura* is a good combination. One can also add potatoes. Spinach is also fried in the same manner. *Khutura xaak* is known to cure diabetes and constipation.

Methi xaak Aru Alu Bhaji
Fenugreek Leaves with Potatoes

Ingredients

Methi *xaak*	:	250 gms
Mustard oil	:	4 tbsps
Chopped garlic	:	1 tbsp
Chillies	:	2
Sliced onion	:	1 medium-sized
Sliced potatoes	:	2 medium-sized
Turmeric powder	:	½ tsp
Salt	:	to taste

Method

§ Clean and chop the methi *xaak*. Sprinkle salt and mix well with the leaves. Keep aside for 10 minutes.
§ Heat the oil in a karai. Add the chopped garlic and chillies. When the garlic changes colour, add the onion and fry till the onions are soft.
§ Add the potatoes and stir for 2 minutes. Add the *xaak*, turmeric powder and cover it. Stir occasionally.
§ When the potatoes are tender, remove the cover. Sprinkle salt if needed. Stir well.
§ Serve *methi xaak aru alu bhaji* with naan or hot chappatis.

The Poa-Mecca and the Hayagriva-Madhab temple of Hajo of the Kamrup district in Assam are famous pilgrimage sites for the followers of Islam and Hindusim respectively.

Patot Diya Tengesi Xaak
Roasted Indian Sorrel

Ingredients

Tengesi xaak (Indian sorrel)	:	100 gms
Banana leaf	:	1
Salt	:	to taste
Mustard oil	:	1 tbsp

Method

§ Take the tender leaves of the *tengesi xaak*. Clean and wash the *xaak*.
§ Clean the banana leaf. Hold it over a low fire to make it pliable.
§ Put the *xaak* on the banana leaf and fold it like a parcel. Tie it with a string.
§ Roast it over slow charcoal fire for a few minutes.
§ Unwrap the parcel. Mix the salt and mustard oil with the roasted *xaak*.
§ Serve tangy *patot diya tengesi xaak* with hot *sewa diya bhat*.

Note: The Indian sorrel is slightly acidic in taste. It is good for diarrhoea and dysentry. It is prescribed for small children in rural areas for its medicinal properties. Diabetic patients should include *tengesi xaak* in their diet.

The Sikh Temple in the Nagaon district is one of the first seats of Sikh faith in Assam.

Bhatot Diya Kolmou Xaak
Swamp Cabbage Boiled with Rice

Ingredients

Kolmou xaak (Swamp cabbage)	:	150 gms
Banana leaf	:	1
Salt	:	to taste
Mustard seed paste	:	1 tbsp
Mustard oil	:	1 tbsp

Method

- Take the tender tendrils of the *kolmou xaak*. Clean and wash them.
- Clean the banana leaf and hold it over a low fire to make it pliable.
- Put the *xaak* on the banana leaf and fold it like a parcel and tie it with a string.
- Boil water in a saucepan. Add the rice and the parcel of *kolmou xaak*. Stir occasionally. By the time the rice is cooked, the *xaak* will also be done.
- Open the parcel and take out the boiled *xaak* in a bowl. Add the salt, mustard seed paste and mustard oil. Mix well.
- Serve *bhatot diya kolmou xaak* with plain rice.

Note: *Kolmou xaak* is known to be a good cure for scabies and heart diseases.

Sajina Phul Aru Haanh Koni Bhaji
Drumstick Flowers with Duck Eggs

Ingredients

Drumstick flowers	:	50 gms
Duck eggs	:	3
Mustard oil	:	4 tbsps
Broken red dry chillies	:	2
Chopped onions	:	2 medium-sized
Finely chopped tomato	:	1 medium-sized
Salt	:	to taste
Cardamom powder	:	½ level tsp
Kharisa	:	1 tbsp

Method

- § Clean and wash the flowers. Beat the eggs well.
- § Heat the mustard oil. Fry the red chillies and chopped onions till the onions change colour.
- § And the drumstick flowers and stir for a minute.
- § Add the chopped tomatoes, salt, beaten eggs and cardamom powder and stir till almost done.
- § Add the *kharisa*. Mix well and remove from the fire.
- § Serve hot *sajina phul aru haanh koni bhaji* with rice, chapattis or parathas.

Note: A typical Assamese *xaak* named *baabori* (a dark green pot herb with a strong smell) is also fried with duck eggs and relished during winter.

Drumstick trees are found in many places of India. All the parts of a drumstick tree have medicinal properties. The flowers of the drumstick tree are known to be good for anaemia. It is rich in vitamins and minerals. These leaves should be included in the diet of nursing mothers. Both the flowers and leaves work as a medicine for tetanus.

Sarioh Botar Lagot Sajina
Drumstick with Mustard Seed Paste

Ingredients

Tender drumsticks	:	250 gms
Mustard oil	:	3 tbsps
Sliced potatoes	:	2 medium-sized
Dry red chillies	:	2
Salt	:	to taste
Turmeric powder	:	½ level tsp
Mustard seed paste	:	2 tbsps
Water	:	400 ml
To garnish	:	green chillies – few mustard oil – 1 tbsp

Method

§ Cut the drumsticks into 1½ inch pieces.
§ Heat the mustard oil in a pan. Add the red chillies, potatoes and drumsticks. Sprinkle salt and turmeric powder. Stir for 2 minutes.
§ Add the mustard seed paste and water. Cover and let it simmer till the drumsticks and potatoes are soft and the gravy is of the desired consistency.
§ Garnish with mustard oil and green chillies.
§ Serve and enjoy *sarioh botar lagot sajina* on a rainy day.

The Rong Ghar, Kareng Ghar, Talatal Ghar and other remnants of Ahom architecture speak volumes about the glorious reign of the Ahom kings in the Sivasagar district of Assam.

Labra Bhaji
Mixed Vegetables

Ingredients

Cauliflower	:	200 gms
Cabbage	:	100 gms
Brinjal	:	100 gms
Pumpkin	:	200 gms
Potatoes	:	200 gms
Onions	:	2 medium-sized
Mustard oil	:	4 tbsps
Panch phuron	:	1 level tsp
Dry red chillies	:	2
Bay leaves	:	2
Turmeric powder	:	1 tsp
Salt	:	to taste

Method

§ Cut the vegetables into medium-sized pieces.
§ Chop the onions.
§ Heat the oil in a karai. Add the *panch phuron*. When the *panch phuron* turns red, add the onions, dry red chillies and bay leaves. Fry till the onions change colour.
§ Add all the vegetables. Sprinkle turmeric powder and salt and stir fry for a minute.
§ Cover it well and reduce the heat. Stir occasionally.

§ Add some water if required. When the vegetables are cooked well, remove it from the fire.
§ Serve hot *labra bhaji* with *khichdi* and pure ghee.

Note: *Labra bhaji* is always served during social functions with *khichdi*.

Mahapurus Srimanta Sankardeva was the founder of the Vaishnavite religion of Assam. He was also a legend in the cultural history of this region, the fountainhead of the Ankiya naat or Bhaona, a form of drama; Bargeet, a form of devotional songs; and the Sattriya dance.

Pur Diya Tetakerela
Stuffed Bittergourd

Ingredients

Tetakerela (Bittergourd)	:	6
Boiled potatoes	:	2 medium-sized
Paneer	:	100 gms
Mustard oil	:	2 tbsps
Finely chopped onions	:	2 medium-sized
Chilli powder	:	½ level tsp
Turmeric powder	:	a pinch
Coriander powder	:	½ tsp
Cumin powder	:	½ tsp
Oil	:	for deep frying
Salt	:	to taste
White thread	:	to tie the stuffed bittergourd

Method

§ Cut the bittergourd into halves, length wise. Rub them with salt and leave for an hour.
§ Wash them well. Remove the pulp with a spoon.
§ Mash the boiled potatoes and paneer well.
§ Heat the oil in a pan. Add the onions. Stir well.
§ When the onions are soft, add the chilli powder, turmeric powder, coriander powder and cumin powder. Also add the mashed paneer and potatoes. Sprinkle salt. Stir for a while.

- Remove from the fire. Stuff the bittergourd with the mashed potato and paneer.
- Place two pieces together and make a whole gourd. Secure with a thread.
- Deep-fry one by one upon moderate heat till done. Soak excess oil with paper napkins.
- Serve hot *pur diya tetakerela* with mint chutney.
- Remove the thread before serving.

Note: Bittergourd is a good antidote to roundworm. It is also good for diabetic patients as it helps in lowering blood and urine sugar levels. The roots are used as a cure for respiratory disorders.

Bilahi Aru Haanh Koni Bhaji
Fried Tomatoes with Duck Eggs

Ingredients

Duck eggs	:	4
Chopped tomatoes	:	6 medium-sized
Mustard oil	:	2 tbsps
Chopped onions	:	2 medium-sized
Slit green chillies	:	2
Chopped coriander leaves	:	2 tbsps
Salt	:	to taste
Pepper	:	a pinch

Method

§ Beat the duck eggs well.
§ Heat the oil in a pan. Add the chopped onions. Sauté till the onions are soft.
§ Add the tomatoes. Stir upon medium heat for a minute. Add the salt and pepper.
§ Add the beaten eggs and the slit green chillies. Stir well.
§ When done, add the chopped coriander. Stir and remove from the fire.
§ Serve *bilahi aru haanh koni bhaji* with *tekeli pitha* (savoury).

Note: The local tomatoes (*bilahi*) are also known as *tenga bengena* in some places of Lower Assam. In some places it is also called *bilati* (foreign) *bengena*, since its origin was not in India.

Kathalor Torkari
Jackfruit Curry

Ingredients

Tender jackfruit (cubed)	:	500 gms
Turmeric powder	:	½ (to boil the jackfruit)
Potatoes (peeled and quartered)	:	3 medium-sized
Sliced tomatoes	:	3 medium-sized
Oil	:	100 ml
Bay leaves	:	2
Onion paste	:	½ cup
Garlic paste	:	½ tbsp
Ginger paste	:	½ tbsp
Cumin seed paste	:	2 tsps
Coriander seed paste	:	2 tsps
Chilli powder	:	1 level tsp
Turmeric power	:	1 level tsp
Warm water	:	250 ml
Garam masala powder	:	1 tsp
Pure ghee	:	½ tbsp
Salt	:	to taste

Method

§ Boil the cubed jackfruit with a little water and turmeric powder. Drain well.

§ Heat the oil in a wok or karai. Half-fry the potatoes and keep them on a paper napkin to drain excess oil.

- § Add the bay leaves to the remaining oil and also add the onion paste. Stir upon medium heat.
- § Add the ginger paste, the garlic paste, the cumin seed paste and the coriander seed paste. Also add the chilli powder. Stir well.
- § When the oil separates, add the turmeric powder, salt, tomatoes, jackfruit and the potatoes.
- § Fry till it becomes golden brown in colour. Add water. Cover and cook upon medium heat till done.
- § Sprinkle the garam masala and mix well. Keep it covered for a while.
- § Remove from the the fire, add the ghee and serve hot *kathalor torkari*.

Note: Jackfruit pickle is very popular among the Assamese people. It is usually eaten with parathas.

Alu Dom
Potato Curry

Ingredients

Boiled potatoes	:	500 gms
Mustard oil	:	100 gms
Bay leaves	:	2
Dry red chillies	:	2
Onion paste	:	½ cup
Garlic paste	:	2 tsps
Ginger paste	:	1 tsp
Chilli powder	:	½ tsp
Pure ghee	:	2 tsps
Turmeric powder	:	½ tsp
Chopped tomatoes	:	3 medium-sized
Hot water	:	400 ml
Cinnamon	:	1 inch long
Green cardamom	:	4
Pure ghee	:	½ tsp
Salt	:	to taste

Method

§ Peel and quarter the potatoes. Make a fine paste of the cinnamon and cardamom.
§ Heat the mustard oil and fry the potatoes till light brown in colour. Keep them aside.
§ In the remaining oil, fry the bay leaves and the dry red chillies.

When they change colour, add the onion paste. Stir upon medium heat for a minute.
§ Add the ginger and garlic paste and stir. Add the chilli powder and pure ghee. Stir well.
§ Sprinkle water a couple of times. When the oil separates, add the chopped tomatoes, fried potatoes, turmeric powder and salt. Stir for about 2 minutes.
§ Add hot water. Cover and let it simmer for 7-8 minutes or till done.
§ Remove the cover. Add pure ghee, the cinnamon and cardamom paste.
§ Stir well. Keep it covered for a minute.
§ Remove it from the fire and serve *alu dom* with *luchi* and chilli pickle.

Tezpur which is situated on the northern bank of the Brahmaputra ,is the home of the hottest variety of chillies of the world which is called 'naga jolokia'.

Jatilao Bhaji
Fried Bottlegourd

Ingredients

Bottlegourd (julienned)	:	500 gms
Mustard oil	:	3 tbsps
Mustard seeds	:	a pinch
Slit green chillies	:	2-3
Salt	:	to taste
Sugar	:	a pinch

Method

§ Heat the oil in a karai. Splutter the mustard seeds in it.
§ Add the bottlegourd, green chillies and salt.
§ Stir and cover. Cook upon medium heat.
§ Stir occasionally. When done, remove from the fire.
§ Serve *jatilao bhaji* with *maachar muri ghonto* and rice.
§ A fried fish head can also be added to the *jatilao bhaji*.

Bottlegourd is also known as panilao. You will find two kinds of bottlegourd in Assam. One is short and the other long. The short one resembles a tekeli (clay pitcher).

Rangalao Bhaji
Fried Pumpkin

Ingredients

Rangalao (pumpkin)	:	750 gms
Mustard oil	:	3 tbsps
Mustard seeds	:	a pinch
Green cardamom	:	3
Dry red chillies	:	2
Bay leaves	:	2
Salt	:	to taste
Sugar	:	½ level tsp

Method

- Peel and clean the pumpkin. Julienne the pumpkin.
- Heat the oil. Splutter the mustard seeds in it and the add the cardamom, chillies and bay leaves. Stir for a few seconds.
- Add the pumpkin, salt and sugar. Stir upon medium fire for a minute.
- Cover and stir occasionally. When soft, remove it from the fire.
- Serve *rangalao bhaji* with plain rice and daal.

Note: This can also be used as a pizza topping along with cheese.

Khowang of the Dibrugarh district of Upper Assam is famous for its pumpkin production.

Alu Koni Pitika
Mashed Potatoes and Eggs

Ingredients

Potatoes	:	4 medium-sized
Eggs	:	2
Finely chopped onion	:	1 medium-sized
Chopped green chillies	:	2
Chopped coriander leaves	:	1 tbsp
Mustard oil	:	1 ½ tsps
Salt	:	to taste

Method

§ Boil and peel the potatoes and eggs.
§ Mash them together, adding the chopped onion, chopped green chillies, chopped coriander leaves, mustard oil and salt.
§ Serve *alu koni pitika* with rice, daal and a piece of lemon.

Note: *Alu koni pitika* with yellow gram daal made with drumstick leaves is a great combination. Instead of boiled eggs, 2 ripe and baked olives can be added, and so can a tablespoon of *kharisa*.

It is said that alu pitika of Assam is so delicious that the British forgot their own recipe of mashed potatoes when they tasted it.

Bengena Pitika
Mashed Brinjal

Ingredients

Brinjals	:	2 large (500 gms)
Mustard oil	:	to rub on the brinjals
Chopped coriander	:	3 tbsps
Julienned ginger	:	according to taste
Chopped green chillies	:	4
Mustard oil	:	1 tbsp
Salt	:	to taste

Method

§ Clean the brinjals. Dry it with a towel. Rub some mustard oil on the brinjals evenly.
§ Roast the brinjals upon slow charcoal fire. They can also be roasted on gas fire. Let then cool and then peel.
§ Mash the pulp after removing the seeds.
§ Add the chopped coriander, julienned ginger, chopped green chillies, mustard oil and salt. Mix well.
§ Serve *bengena pitika* with rice and *ada diya mogur dail*.
§ Roasted brinjal also tastes great if it is mashed and mixed well with salt, a little pure ghee and grated ginger.

On the border of Arunachal Pradesh lies Bhalukpong. Its landscape takes one's breath away with its rich bio-diversity and scenic beauty.

Manxo
Meat/Poultry

The day I looked forward to as a kid was Sunday. Besides being a holiday when I didn't have to wake up at dawn to get ready, it was the day when *sagoli manxo* (mutton) would be cooked at home. So the afternoon meal became the most anticipated occasion of the day. And an occasion it was. My father would dart off to the market to get the freshest and the best of the meat. And because almost every family in the locality would be doing the same, if one was a little late, there would be no meat left in the market. By the time my father would be back from the market, the other ingredients would be ready. The potatoes neatly peeled, tomatoes and onions sliced, ginger and cardamom ground and the masalas sorted out. If there was a feast or during Bihu, mutton would always be on the menu.

In the villages, poultry farms are a common sight. Duck meat is preferred to mutton and used in recipes for starters. In parts of Lower Assam like Barpeta, pigeon meat with pepper is quite popular, and is especially served to guests.

Meat, though popular, is not a part of the regular Assamese diet. The Ahoms who ruled Assam for over six hundred years since the thirteenth century, had various pork recipes. In the regions of Buddhist influence and tantric dominance, meat was popular, but it usually came in the wake of sacrificial rites. In the past, various communities of Assam prepared the occasional hunted deer.

Lamb, duck, pigeon, chicken and pork are all part of Assamese cuisine. Pork is more popular amongst the ethnic tribes. Though broiler chicken is available, people still prefer country chicken.

Patha Manxor Jhul
Mutton Curry

Ingredients

Mutton (cut into 1 inch cubes)	:	1 kg
Potatoes	:	4 medium-sized
Vinegar	:	2 tbsps
Sliced onions	:	3 large sized
Mustard oil	:	2 tbsps (to marinate the meat)
Turmeric powder	:	1 tsp
Salt	:	1 level tsp
Mustard oil	:	4 tbsps
Sugar	:	½ level tsp
Bay leaves	:	4
Onion paste	:	½ cup
Ginger paste	:	1 tbsp
Garlic paste	:	2 tbsps
Cumin seed paste	:	1 tsp
Coriander seed paste	:	1 tsp
Chilli powder	:	1 tsp
Sliced tomatoes	:	4 medium-sized
Warm water	:	400 ml
Cinnamon sticks	:	2 (1 inch each)
Green cardamom	:	8
Cloves	:	6
Pure ghee	:	1 tsp
Salt	:	to taste

Method

- Clean the mutton. Add the vinegar, sliced onions, mustard oil, turmeric powder and salt to the mutton. Mix well and cover. Marinate for an hour.
- Peel the potatoes and quarter them.
- Heat the oil in a pressure cooker. Caramelise some sugar.
- Add the bay leaves. Stir. Add the onion paste and stir continuously for a minute.
- Add the ginger paste, garlic paste, cumin seed paste and coriander seed paste to the fried onion paste and stir. Sprinkle some water while frying.
- When the oil floats to the top, add the chilli powder and potatoes. Stir for a minute.
- Add the marinated mutton and sliced tomatoes and stir.
- When the mutton dries up add the salt and water.
- Close the cooker. Bring the pressure cooker to full pressure on high heat.
- Reduce the heat and cook for 12 minutes.
- Let it cool. Powder the cinnamon, cardamom and cloves and add it to the mutton. Also add the pure ghee.
- Stir and cover the *patha manxor jhul* for 2 minutes.
- Serve it hot with *sewa diya bhat* on a banana leaf.

Shanmehali Xaakor Lagot Patha Manxo
Mutton with Mixed Herbs

Ingredients

Mutton (cut into serving portions)	:	1 kg
Turmeric powder	:	1 level tsp
Warm water	:	400 gms
Mustard leaves *(sarioh xaak)*	:	100 gms
Spinach *(paleng xaak)*	:	100 gms
Drumstick leaves *(sajina pat)*	:	50 gms
Fenugreek leaves *(methi xaak)*	:	25 gms
Coriander leaves *(dhania xaak)*	:	25 gms
Sorrel *(suka xaak)*	:	50 gms
Mustard oil	:	6 tbsps
Sliced onions	:	4 medium-sized
Slit green chillies	:	5
Garlic paste	:	2 tbsps
Ginger paste	:	1 tbsp
Salt and pepper	:	to taste

Method

§ Wash the mutton and drain excess water.
§ Clean the mustard leaves, spinach, drumstick, fenugreek and sorrel leaves. Chop the leaves.
§ Put the mutton in a pressure cooker with the water and turmeric powder. Bring the cooker to full pressure and reduce the heat. After 7 minutes, remove the cooker from the fire.

§ Open the pressure cooker and put it upon the fire and keep stirring till the meat is dry.
§ In a karai, heat the mustard oil. Add the sliced onions and green chillies. Stir for a minute and add the garlic and ginger paste. Stir till the onions start to get brown.
§ Add the chopped *xaak*, mutton and sprinkle salt. Stir upon moderate heat.
§ When the *xaak* disintegrates and mixes with the meat, increase the heat and stir for a minute.
§ Sprinkle some freshly ground pepper and serve *sanmehali xaakor lagot patha manxo* with sticky rice.

Patha Manxor Korma
Mutton Korma

Ingredients

Mutton (cut into serving portions)	:	1 kg
Raw papaya paste	:	200 gms
Curd	:	350 gms
Mustard oil	:	100 ml
Cinnamon sticks	:	2 (1 inch pieces)
Cardamoms (green)	:	8
Cloves	:	4
Sliced onions	:	3 medium-sized
Garlic paste	:	2 tbsps
Ginger paste	:	1 tbsp
Onion paste	:	½ cup
Chilli powder	:	1 tsp
Warm water	:	500 ml
Poppy seed paste	:	2 tbsps
Blanched almond paste	:	2 tbsps
Coconut milk	:	200 ml
Salt	:	to taste
To garnish	:	*maan dhania* or fresh chillies

Method

§ Clean and wash the mutton. Marinate it with the papaya paste and curd for an hour.

- § Heat the oil in a karai and fry the cinnamon, cardamom, cloves and the sliced onions.
- § When the onions are slightly brown in colour, add the garlic paste, ginger paste and onion paste. Also sprinkle the chilli powder.
- § Fry upon a medium fire. Sprinkle water a couple of times while frying.
- § When the oil floats to the top, add the meat. Let the meat simmer in its own juices upon medium heat. Sprinkle salt to taste.
- § When the meat is dry, add water and cook till the meat is tender. Add more water if required.
- § Mix the poppy seeds and almond paste with coconut milk and add it to the mutton.
- § Let it simmer upon low heat till the oil appears on the top.
- § Serve *patha manxor korma* garnished with coriander leaves or fresh chillies.

Baanhgajor Lagot Kukura
Chicken with Bamboo Shoot

Ingredients

Dressed country chicken	:	750 gms
Baanhgaj (tender bamboo shoot)	:	300 gms
Mustard oil	:	100 ml
Chopped onions	:	4 medium-sized
Ginger paste	:	1 tsp
Dry red chilli paste	:	1 tbsp
Turmeric powder	:	1 level tsp
Chopped tomatoes	:	4 medium-sized
Hot water	:	300 ml
Green cardamom	:	8 (coarsely ground)
Thick coconut milk	:	200 ml
Salt	:	to taste
To garnish	:	a few mint leaves

Method

§ Cut the chicken into 2 inch pieces. Clean the chicken.
§ Wash the fresh bamboo shoot. Soak it in water for 30 minutes. Drain and slice it.
§ Heat the oil in a heavy-bottomed pan. Add the chopped onions. Stir well.
§ When the onions are soft, add the ginger and chilli paste. Stir. When the oil separates and floats to the top, add the turmeric powder and chicken.

Jyoti Das

- § Stir the chicken for about 8 minutes. Add the tomatoes and the bamboo shoot and stir for 5 minutes.
- § Add hot water, the cardamom and the salt. Lower the heat, cover it and let it simmer till the chicken is tender and dry.
- § Add the coconut milk and stir continuously till the oil separates and appears on the top.
- § Garnish it with mint leaves and serve. *Baanhgajor lagot kukura* is a rich mouth-watering authentic recipe.

Note: To make red chilli paste, slit red dry chillies and remove the seeds. Soak in warm water for 5 minutes. Wash well and make a fine paste.

Paleng Xaakot Kukura
Chicken with Spinach

Ingredients

Chicken (dressed)	:	500 gms (8 pieces)
Coriander seed paste	:	½ tsp
Cumin seed paste	:	½ tsp
Green cinnamon (crushed)	:	3
Spinach leaves *(paleng xaak)*	:	250 gms
Mustard oil	:	3 tbsps
Bay leaves	:	2
Cumin seed	:	a pinch
Chopped onion	:	1 medium-sized
Dry red chillies	:	2
Hot water	:	200 ml
Milk	:	100 ml
Freshly powdered pepper	:	½ tsp
Salt and sugar	:	to taste

Method

§ Clean the chicken pieces. Add the coriander seed paste, cumin seed paste and crushed cinnamon to the chicken. Mix well and marinate for 10 minutes.
§ Steam the chicken. Keep the chicken juice aside.
§ Blanch the spinach leaves in hot water for a minute. Cool with chilled water to retain the fresh green colour. Drain and make a smooth paste in a mixie.

- § Heat the mustard oil. Add the bay leaves and cumin seeds. When the seeds become red, add the chopped onions and dry chillies. Stir well.
- § When the onions are soft, add the chicken pieces.
- § Stir the chicken pieces for a minute. Add the spinach paste, hot water and the chicken juice. Remove the red dry chillies.
- § Let it simmer for 2 minutes. Add the milk. Sprinkle salt, pepper and sugar to taste.
- § Remove from the fire when the gravy thickens and serve *paleng xaakot kukura* with rice baked in bamboo hollows.

Jalukia Kukura
Chicken with Pepper

Ingredients

Dressed country chicken	:	1 kg
Oil	:	5 tbsps
Bay leaves	:	3
Chopped onions	:	4 medium-sized
Ginger (julienned)	:	1 tbsp
Turmeric powder	:	1 level tsp
Fresh pepper paste	:	1½ tbsps
Chopped tomatoes	:	4 medium-sized
Warm water	:	400 ml
Salt	:	to taste

Method

§ Cut the chicken into 1 inch pieces. Clean the chicken.
§ Heat the oil. Add the bay leaves and the chopped onions. Fry the onions upon medium heat and keep stirring till the onions change colour.
§ Add the chicken pieces, ginger, turmeric powder, salt and stir for 5 minutes. Add the pepper paste. Stir for a while.
§ Add the chopped tomatoes. Stir till dry.
§ Add water and let it boil. Reduce the heat, cover it and let it simmer upon a low flame.
§ When the chicken is tender, remove *jalukia kukura* from the fire. Relish this dish on a cold rainy day with chapattis.

It is one of the favourite recipes of the people of Assam during cold and wet winter nights, and is specially made if someone is suffering from a cold.

Kukurar Lagot Ada
Chicken with Ginger

Ingredients

Chicken (dressed)	:	1 kg
Rice	:	3 tbsps
Warm water	:	600 ml
Green chillies	:	6
Ginger paste	:	1½ tbsps
Salt	:	to taste

Method

- Cut the chicken into pieces and clean it.
- Clean the rice and soak in water for 30 minutes. Drain.
- Heat a heavy karai. Stir the chicken pieces upon medium heat continuously for a minute. Cover it.
- Cook till the chicken is dry, stirring occasionally.
- Add 600 ml of warm water and increase the heat. Also add the rice. Stir for awhile.
- Add the green chillies and cover. Let it simmer on medium heat till the rice is soft.
- Remove the cover. Add the ginger paste and salt and keep stirring till the gravy thickens.
- Serve *kukurar lagot ada* with steamed rice.

The above recipe is a favourite dish of people of the Bodo community and is called aksa pok.

Rasal Kukura
Juicy Chicken

Ingredients

Chicken (broiler)	:	1 kg
Onions	:	4 medium-sized
Ginger	:	30 gms
Dry red chillies	:	5
Mustard oil	:	4 tbsps
Bay leaves	:	2
Cinnamon	:	1 inch piece
Green cardamom	:	4
Rice powder	:	1 tsp
Warm water	:	600 ml
Pure ghee	:	1 level tsp
Turmeric powder	:	½ level tsp
Salt	:	to taste
To garnish	:	fried dry chillies

Method

§ Clean the chicken. Remove the skin and cut it into pieces.
§ Grate the onions and take out the juice. Crush the ginger and take out the juice.
§ Marinate the chicken pieces with salt, onions and ginger juice for an hour.
§ Slit the dry red chillies and remove the seeds. Wash it with warm water and make a fine paste.

§ In a thick-bottomed pan, heat the mustard oil. Add the bay leaves, cinnamon and green cardamom. Stir fry for half a minute.
§ Add the salt, turmeric powder and the chicken pieces. Keep the marinated juice aside. Also add the chilli paste.
§ Let it cook on high heat for about 5 minutes. Add warm water and the marinated chicken juice and bring to boil. Reduce the heat.
§ Let it simmer till the chicken is almost done. Mix the rice powder with a little water and add to the chicken. Stir for a minute.
§ Add the pure ghee and mix well. Cover and remove the pan from the heat.
§ Serve hot *rasal kukura* with *joha* rice.

Note: Potatoes can also be added to this dish.

Kumura Aru Haanh
Duck Curry with White Pumpkin

Ingredients

Dressed duck	:	1 kg
Kumura (white pumpkin)	:	500 gms
Potatoes	:	4 medium-sized
Mustard oil	:	100 ml
Chopped onions	:	4 medium-sized
Garlic paste	:	2 tbsps
Ginger paste	:	1 tbsp
Bay leaves	:	4
Coriander powder	:	1 tsp
Cumin powder	:	1 tsp
Green slit chillies	:	4
Turmeric powder	:	1 tsp
Garam masala powder	:	1 tsp
Hot water	:	1 litre
Salt	:	to taste
Pepper	:	to taste

Method

§ Cut the duck into serving portions. Peel the *kumura* and the potatoes and cut into pieces.
§ Heat the oil in a karai. Fry the onions till soft. Add the garlic and ginger paste.
§ Stir upon medium heat till the oil separates and floats to the top. Sprinkle water to prevent it from sticking to the karai.

- § Add the duck meat, bay leaves, coriander powder and cumin powder. Also add the *kumura*, potatoes, slit green chillies and turmeric powder, one by one.
- § Stir continuously till the oil separates and the meat is dry.
- § Add water and sprinkle garam masala and salt. Cover and let it simmer upon a low fire till the meat is tender.
- § Add the pepper. Serve *kumura aru haanh* curry with sticky rice or *joha* rice and enjoy it on a banana leaf.

During the feasts in rural areas, duck curry with kumura (white pumpkin) is specially served during winter. An honoured guest is always welcomed with this curry and sticky rice in Upper Assam.

Bhoja Haanh
Duck Fry

Ingredients

Oil	:	for deep frying
Dressed duck	:	1 kg
Garlic paste	:	1 tbsp
Ginger paste	:	½ tbsp
Red dry chilli paste	:	½ tbsp
Vinegar	:	2 tbsps
Cumin seed paste	:	1 tsp
Turmeric powder	:	1 tsp
Pepper	:	1 tsp
Salt	:	to taste

Method

§ Make 1 inch pieces of the duck meat and drain the excess water.
§ Mix the pieces with the ginger paste, garlic paste and red chilli paste. Also mix the vinegar, cumin seed paste, turmeric powder and salt. Marinate for 2 hours.
§ In a heavy karai, heat the mustard oil for deep frying. Fry 8-10 pieces at a time till they become golden brown in colour.
§ Sprinkle pepper powder and serve hot *bhoja haanh* with *kharisa* chutney or mint chutney.

Duck fry is specially served during the Bihu feast as an appetiser with tea or laopani (rice beer)

Paro Manxor Jhul
Pigeon Curry

Ingredients

Pigeons (dressed)	:	4
Oil	:	100 ml
Grated onions	:	4 medium-sized
Ginger paste	:	1 tbsp
Garlic paste	:	2 tbsps
Slit green chillies	:	4
Coriander powder	:	1 tsp
Cumin powder	:	1 tsp
Turmeric powder	:	¾ tsp
Freshly ground pepper	:	1½ tsps
Warm water	:	600 ml
Salt	:	to taste

Method

- Cut the pigeon meat into pieces and wash it.
- Heat the oil in a karai. Fry the grated onions till they change colour.
- Add the ginger and garlic paste. Stir upon medium heat.
- When the oil floats to the top, add the meat and the slit green chillies. Also add the coriander powder, cumin powder and turmeric powder. Stir upon medium heat.
- When the pigeon meat becomes dry and golden brown in colour, add the water.

- § Sprinkle the salt and bring it to boil. Cover and let it simmer till the meat is tender.
- § Add the freshly ground pepper. When the gravy thickens, remove the curry from the fire.
- § Enjoy *paro manxor jhul* with rice on a rainy day.

Phola Mati Dailor Lagot Gahori
Pork with Split Black Gram

Ingredients

Pork	:	500 gms
Split black gram	:	200 gms
Mustard oil	:	5 tbsps
Sliced onions	:	4 medium-sized
Crushed ginger	:	1½ tbsps
Crushed garlic	:	2 tbsps
Slit green chillies	:	6
Hot water	:	1 litre
Turmeric powder	:	½ tsp
Salt	:	to taste

Method

§ Soak the black gram for 3 hours. Wash it well.
§ Wash the pork, and cut into 1½ inch pieces.
§ Heat the mustard oil in a heavy-bottomed pan. Add the sliced onions and stir fry upon moderate heat till the onions are soft.
§ Add the crushed ginger, garlic and chillies to it and stir.
§ When the onions turns brown, add the pork. Stir fry the pork for about 10 minutes.
§ Add the black gram, turmeric powder and salt to the pan.
§ Continue stirring for a few more minutes on high heat.
§ Add hot water and cover.

- § Let it simmer for 15 minutes or until the pork is completely cooked.
- § Remove the pan from the fire and let it cool.
- § Serve hot *phola mati dailor lagot gahori* with rice and *kharisa*.

Note: If the split daal sticks to the pan while frying and a slightly burnt smell emanates, gives an authentic flavour and aroma to the dish.

The above dish is very popular amongst the Mising and Deori people of Majuli. Majuli, which is a river island of the Brahmaputra, is considered to be one of the biggest river islands of the world. In their feasts, the Mising and Deori tribes serve this dish.

Pithagurir Lagot Gahori Manxo
Pork with Rice Powder

Ingredients

Pork	:	500 gms
Mustard oil	:	2 tbsps
Chopped onions	:	2 medium-sized
Crushed garlic	:	1 tbsp
Crushed ginger	:	1 tbsp
Green chillies	:	4
Warm water	:	200 ml
Rice powder	:	2½ tbsps
Water	:	300 ml
Turmeric powder	:	½ level tsp
Salt	:	to taste

Method

§ Clean, wash and cut the meat into 1½ inch cubes.
§ Heat the oil in a heavy karai. Add the onions and stir for a minute. Add the ginger, garlic, green chillies and the pork. Stir fry upon medium heat for about 15 minutes.
§ Sprinkle turmeric powder and salt. Stir for a minute and add warm water.
§ Cover and let it simmer upon low heat for about half an hour.
§ Mix the rice powder with water and pour it into the karai. Stir continuously so that no lumps are formed.
§ When the gravy thickens, remove the karai from the fire.
§ Serve *pithagurir lagot gahori manxo* with rice.

Baanhgajor Lagot Gahori
Pork With Bamboo Shoot

Ingredients

Pork	:	500 gms
Chopped onions	:	3 medium-sized
Ginger paste	:	1 tbsp
Garlic paste	:	1½ tbsps
Turmeric powder	:	½ level tsp
Chilli powder	:	1 tsp
Slit green chillies	:	3
Fermented bamboo shoot	:	3 tbsps
Warm water	:	200 ml
Salt	:	to taste

Method

§ Clean and cut the pork into serving portions.
§ Heat a heavy-bottomed pan on a medium fire. Put the pork pieces into and and cover.
§ Stir occasionally till the fat comes out and the meat turns brown.
§ Take the pork out of the pan. In the fat of the pork, fry the chopped onions, ginger and garlic paste.
§ When it turns brown, add the turmeric powder, chilli powder, salt and the pork. Fry for a while.
§ Add the bamboo shoot and the slit green chillies. Stir for a minute.

§ Transfer the pork to a small pressure cooker and add warm water.
§ Bring the pressure cooker to full pressure and reduce the heat.
§ Keep the pressure cooker upon the fire for about 15 minutes.
§ Let it cool and serve *baanhgajor lagot gahori* with rice.

Note: Tribal villagers heat a heavy-bottomed pan on firewood and cook 4-5 kgs pork on slow fire till the pork turns brown and the fat of the pork seeps out. They use this fat in various recipes. The cooked pork can be stored for a few days and used whenever required.

Maach
Fish

The word fish conjures up different images in my mind: our backyard pond, small puddles surrounded by over-zealous children during the monsoon, the Kolong of Nagaon district, the Dihing river of Upper Assam and the mighty Brahmaputra. I vividly remember our backyard pond, which was always teeming with *dorikona, muwa, kaawai, goroi and puthi* fish. And whenever a guest would visit, Ramu dada would head towards the pond with his excited entourage, which included my brothers, cousins and myself. Equipped with a *khaloi* or a *jakoi*, he would get down to the business of catching the fish. And we would watch the action, totally mesmerised. Occasionally we had a chance to join the party. If my father was in a particularly good mood, we were allowed to catch one or two with small fishing rods. But we would not allow our catch to be served to the guest. We would relish the spoils ourselves. We considered our catch a trophy rather than something to be eaten. It surprises me till today how easily the fish could be fooled to take the bait. No sooner did we dip the rod, a fish would come up, hooked to it. And eventually, the fresh fish out of the pond would be fried and served as a starter to the guest and the family. During the monsoons, fishing almost became a daily ritual, when fish from the overflowing river would unwittingly come to swarm the inundated land.

I have also grown up watching my father catch fish with a sharp bamboo pole or *jakoi* (a bamboo net tied to a triangular frame). He would scoop out the fish with a *jakoi* in a single dip.

Earlier, every Assamese household had a pond in the backyard filled with fish. But with time, especially in cities, due to modernisation and paucity of time and space, people have started buying fish from vendors, who pour in from nearby villages to sell their catch.

Assamese people as a whole are fish lovers. Every meal in Assam is served with rice and nothing compliments it better than fish. No meal is complete without fish in some form or the other. Though they prefer fresh fish, small or large, usually caught in their backyard pond or in the purling creek that runs through the village or rivers and its tributaries, the supply cannot meet the demand and they have to settle for 'fresh frozen' varieties. Group fishing is common in the villages during the *ujaan* of fish (act of coming out of fish in large numbers). Men and women of all ages and children, fishing with excitement by the river side or ponds is a common sight during this season. Dried and fermented fish is equally popular among the ethnic communities. Fish preparations are usually *tenga* (sour) or *adkhoriya*. The souring agents are usually lemon or lime, cocum, elephant apple, Chinese date palm, tamarind, sour tomatoes (*tenga begena*), olives, hog plum, fermented bamboo shoot (*kharisa*) and various sour herbs. People of Upper Assam enjoy fish *tenga* more than those of Lower Assam.

Though *adkhoriya* is a fish preparation which is not sour, a curry seasoned with alkali is also called *adkhoriya* in some places. In the Barpeta area of Lower Assam, fish curry prepared with ginger (*ada*) is also called *adkhoriya*.

Fresh fish in the *tenga* makes it delicious on a hot sunny day. It also keeps the body cool.

Baked fish, whether baked in an open fire or a bamboo hollow or in a banana leaf is the most popular fish preparation of Assamese cuisine.

Pitha Gurir Lagot Sijua Maach
Boiled Fish with Rice Powder

Ingredients

Boneless fish	:	1 kg (10 pieces)
Rice powder	:	80 gms
Water	:	900 ml
Green chillies	:	5
Turmeric powder	:	1 tsp
Salt	:	to taste
To garnish	:	A small bunch of coriander leaves

Method

§ Clean the fish.
§ Coarsely chop the coriander leaves.
§ Boil the fish in a pan in 700 ml of boiling water.
§ Break the chillies. Add the chillies, turmeric powder and salt to the boiling fish.
§ Make a mixture of the rice powder and 200 ml of water. When the fish pieces are almost done, add the rice powder mixture to it. Stir continuously so that no lumps are formed.
§ When the gravy thickens, add the coriander leaves. Cover and remove the pan from the fire.
§ Serve hot *pitha gurir lagot sijua maach* with *bora chaulor bhat*.

Variation – Chicken can also be used in place of fish. The chicken must be half-fried before it is added to the boiling water.

The Mising people use fresh boneless fish like borali (Wallago attu), bosa (Eutropicthys vacha) and nariya (Clupisoma garua) in this dish.

Kharisar Rasot Bhoja Magur Maach
Cat Fish Fried in Bamboo Shoot Juice

Ingredients

Magur maach (cat fish)	:	3 (500 gms)
Salt	:	1 level tsp
Turmeric powder	:	1 ½ level tsps
Mustard oil	:	4 tbsps
Fenugreek seed	:	a pinch
Slit green chillies	:	2
Sliced onions	:	2 medium-sized
Bamboo shoot juice	:	3 tbsps
Salt	:	as desired
To garnish	:	A sliced radish
		A sliced carrot
		coriander leaves

Method

§ Clean and wash the fish. Make four incisions on both sides of the fish.
§ Rub the fish with salt and turmeric powder. Keep it covered for 15 minutes.
§ Heat the oil in a frying pan and fry the fish till it is half done. Keep it on a paper napkin to soak excess oil.
§ Add the fenugreek seeds and chillies to the remaining oil in the pan. Also add the sliced onions and the fried fish.

- Fry the fish upon a low fire for 5 minutes. Add the bamboo shoot juice. Stir.
- Put the fish on a plate and bake in a hot oven for 10 minutes.
- Garnish the fish with sliced radish, carrots and coriander leaves. Serve hot.
- *Kharisar rasot bhoja magur maach* can be served as a first course in a typical Assamese sit-down lunch or dinner.

Magur maach is a type of mud water fish which is black in colour. Its scientific name is Clarius assamensis.

Maachor Kalia
Fish Kalia

Ingredients

Kaawai maach	:	½ kg (6-8 pieces)
Salt	:	1 level tsp
Turmeric powder	:	½ level tsp
Mustard oil	:	to fry the fish
Dry red chillies	:	4
Mustard oil	:	3 tbsps
Bay leaves	:	3
Onion paste	:	4 tbsps
Curd (beaten)	:	50 ml
Turmeric powder	:	½ tsp
Chopped tomatoes	:	2 medium-sized
Raisin paste	:	1 tbsp
Hot water	:	300 ml
Salt	:	to taste
Sugar	:	to taste
To garnish	:	sliced tomatoes 1 red fresh chilli

Method

§ Clean and wash the fish.
§ Make three incisions on both sides of each fish. Rub the fish with salt and turmeric powder.
§ Fry the fish till half done in mustard oil in a karai.

- § Remove the seeds of the dry chillies. Wash it with warm water and make a fine paste.
- § Heat fresh oil in a karai. Add the bay leaves and the onion paste. Fry for a minute.
- § Add the chilli paste and stir continuously. Sprinkle water a couple of times.
- § Add the curd and stir.
- § When the oil separates and floats to the top, add the turmeric powder, chopped tomatoes, raisin paste, sugar and salt. Stir.
- § When the tomatoes are soft, add hot water.
- § Let it boil. Add the fish and cover.
- § Let it simmer till the gravy thickens and the fish is soft.
- § Garnish *kaawai maachor kalia* with sliced tomatoes and a fresh red chilli.
- § Serve hot with rice.

Note: Though it is not an Assamese dish, I have seen it being prepared at home from my early childhood days whenever my father would bring home fresh *kaawai* fish.

The scientific name of the kaawai fish is Anabas scandens.

Maach Pitika
Mashed Fish

Ingredients

Boneless fish *(ari)*	:	500 gms (8 pieces)
Banana leaf	:	1
Mustard oil	:	2 tbsps
Chopped onions	:	2 medium-sized
Chopped coriander leaves	:	one small bunch
Chopped green chillies	:	2
Salt	:	to taste

Method

§ Clean and dry the banana leaf. Hold it over a low fire to make it pliable.
§ Put the boneless fish pieces on the banana leaf. Fold it like a parcel and tie it with a string.
§ Place the parcel over a hot griddle over medium heat.
§ Roast both sides till you get the aroma of the burnt leaf and the baked fish.
§ Remove the parcel from the griddle. Let it cool. Open the parcel and take out the baked fish.
§ Mash the fish with mustard oil, chopped coriander leaves, chopped onions, chopped green chillies and salt.
§ Serve the *maach pitika* with rice and *dail*.
§ 2 tsps of *kharisa* chutney can be added to the *maach pitika*.

Note: Maach pitika can be used in a sandwich.

The scientific name of ari fish is Aorichthys seenghala.

Bhapot Diya Elihi Maach
Steamed Hilsa Fish

Ingredients

Elihi maach	:	10 pieces
Mustard seeds	:	1½ tbsps
Slit green chillies	:	4
Finely chopped onions	:	3 medium-sized
Mustard oil	:	2 tbsps
Salt	:	to taste
To garnish	:	mustard oil – 2 tbsps
		few green chillies

Method

§ Clean and wash the fish.
§ Make a fine paste of the mustard seeds with a little salt.
§ Mix the fish with the mustard seed paste, slit green chillies, chopped onions, mustard oil and salt in a bowl.
§ Marinate for 5 minutes. Steam it for half an hour or until done.
§ Garnish it with mustard oil and green chillies.
§ Serve hot *bhapot diya elihi maach* with rice and enhance its taste with few drops of fresh mustard oil and green chillies.

Elihi fish is available in the Brahmaputra. But the fish-loving Assamese people prefer the elihi fish of the Podda river which is tastier.

Baanhor Chungat Maach
Fish in a Bamboo Hollow

Ingredients

Saru maach (small fish)	:	350 gms
Sliced onions	:	2 small-sized
Chopped green chillies	:	3
Kharisa	:	2 tbsps
Mustard oil	:	1 tbsp
Salt	:	to taste
Tender bamboo hollow	:	2
Banana leaves	:	2
To garnish	:	coriander leaves mustard oil

Method

§ Clean and wash the fish thoroughly.
§ Mix the sliced onions, chopped chillies, *kharisa*, mustard oil and salt in a small bowl.
§ Add the mixture to the fish. Mix well and marinate for 10 minutes.
§ Fill the bamboo hollows with the marinated fish and then seal them with the banana leaves.
§ Place the hollows over a charcoal fire. Rotate the bamboo hollows from time to time till they are evenly burnt. Let them cool.
§ Slit open the bamboo hollows and empty the fish into a serving plate.

§ Garnish with fresh mustard oil and coriander leaves.
§ Serve *baanhor chungat maach* with fresh green chillies.

The fish I prefer to use in the above recipe is called muwa maach in Assam and its scientific name is Ambly pharyrodon molan. It can be fried and served as a starter.

Patot Dia Maach – 1
Baked Fish in a Banana Leaf – 1

Ingredients

Small fish	:	8 (4 inches in length)
Mustard seeds	:	1 tbsp
Mint chutney	:	2 tbsps
Chopped onions	:	1 medium-sized
Mustard oil	:	2 tbsps
Salt	:	to taste
Banana leaves	:	4
To garnish	:	tomato slices
		The flowers of spring onion
		The stems of spring onions

Method

- Clean the fish. Make a paste of the mustard seeds and add a pinch of salt.
- Rub the fish with salt.
- Fill the stomach of the fish with the mustard seed paste and keep it covered for 5 minutes.
- Mix the mustard oil, chopped onions and mint chutney in a small bowl and rub it on the fish.
- Clean the banana leaves and wipe them dry. Hold them over a low fire to make them pliable. Cut the leaves into the desired size.
- Put 2 of the small fishes on each banana leaf. Fold the leaves like an envelope and tie them with strings.

- § Grease a baking tray with oil and put the four envelopes on the tray.
- § Bake in a preheated oven at 150°C for 30-35 minutes or till done.
- § Open the parcels and serve *patot dia maach* garnished with tomatoes, spring onion flowers and stems on a banana leaf.

Note: Traditionally this dish is prepared over a low charcoal fire.

Patot Dia Dorikona Maach – 2

Baked Fish In a Banana Leaf – 2

Ingredients

Dorikona maach	:	300 gms
Banana leaf	:	1
Chopped tender spinach	:	100 gms
Chopped onions	:	2 medium-sized
Freshly chopped ginger	:	1 tsp
Chopped green chillies	:	1 tsp
Lemon juice	:	1 tbsp
Mustard oil	:	1 tbsp
Salt	:	to taste
To garnish	:	chopped cabbage chopped coriander leaves

Method

§ Clean the small *dorikona maach*.
§ Clean the banana leaf. Dry it and hold it over a low fire to make the leaf pliable.
§ Mix the chopped spinach, onions, ginger and green chillies. Also add the lemon juice. Mix them in a bowl with your fingers.
§ Add the small fish, mustard oil and salt to the bowl and mix well.
§ Put the fish along with the mixed ingredients on the banana leaf and wrap it into a parcel.
§ Secure the parcel with a string. Place the parcel over a griddle on moderate heat.

- Roast both sides till you get the aroma of the burnt leaf and baked fish.
- Remove the parcel from the fire. Open the parcel and lay the fish on a plate and garnish with the chopped coriander leaves and cabbage.
- Serve *patot diya dorikona maach* with fresh mustard oil, green chillies and lemon juice.
- *Dorikona* baked with the herb *mosundari* (Houttuynia cordata) is a popular delicacy.

The scientific name of the small dorikona fish is Rasbora daniconius.
Any variety of small fish can be baked similarly.

Sukan Maachor Gura
Ground Dry Fish

Ingredients

Fresh fish (small)	:	1 kg
Salt	:	40 gms
Bamboo hollows	.:	2

Method

- Clean and wash the small fish.
- Also clean and dry the bamboo hollows.
- Dry the fish in the sun for 4-5 days.
- When completely dry, add salt and grind it.
- Put it in bamboo hollows and seal the mouths tightly.
- Serve *sukan maachor gura* as a special dish.
- It can be stored for a month.

This is a dish of the Tai Phakes of Upper Assam and is made for special occasions. They call it pānāo.

The Tai Phakes also make dry meat similarly. They call it Ngu Hāing.

Kosu Pator Lagot Saru Maach
Small Fish with Colocasia Leaves

Ingredients

Bamboo hollows	:	3
Banana leaves	:	3
Kosu pat (colocasia leaves)	:	400 gms
Small river fish	:	1 kg
Slit green chillies	:	6
Salt	:	to taste

Method

§ Clean the bamboo hollows.
§ Collect the colocasia leaves on a sunny day.
§ Clean and wash the fish. Dry it in the sun for a day. Turn the fish thrice while drying.
§ Coarsely grind the colocasia leaves, fish, green chillies and salt.
§ Stuff the fish mixture in the bamboo hollows. Seal the mouths of the hollows with banana leaves.
§ Keep aside for a month.
§ Relish authentic *kosu pator lagot saru maach* as a side dish or with rice.

Note: The above dish is called napam by the people of the Bodo community.

Outengar Maachor Tenga
Elephant Apple Fish Tenga

Ingredients

Rohu fish	:	10 pieces
Oil	:	for frying the fish
Salt and turmeric powder	:	to rub the fish pieces with
Ripe elephant apple (*outenga*)	:	½
Water (to boil the *outenga*)	:	300 ml
Sliced tomatoes	:	750 gms
Julienned bottlegourd	:	350 gms
Mustard oil	:	1 tbsp
Fenugreek seeds	:	a pinch
Turmeric powder	:	1 level tsp
Hot water	:	800 ml
Lemon juice	:	2 tbsps
Salt and sugar	:	to taste
To garnish	:	green chillies – 4 chopped coriander leaves – 1 tbsp

Method

§ Clean the fish. Drain and rub it well with salt and turmeric powder. Keep it covered for 5 minutes.

§ Remove the thick outer layer and inner core of the *outenga*. Cut the middle layer of the *outenga* into 1 inch pieces. Clean and pound the pieces to make it soft.

- Pressure cook the *outenga* for 5 minutes in 300 ml of water.
- Heat the oil in a karai. Fry the fish pieces till half done and keep them on a paper napkin to drain the excess oil.
- Heat 1 tbsp of fresh oil and add the fenugreek seeds. When the seeds turn black, remove them from the oil.
- Add the sliced tomatoes and the julienned bottlegourd. Sprinkle turmeric powder and salt. Cover and let it cook upon moderate heat till the bottleground is soft.
- Add the *outenga* with the juice and the hot water to the karai.
- Let it boil and simmer for about 8 minutes. Add the fish and let it simmer till the fish is soft. Sprinkle the sugar. Stir well. Add the lemon juice.
- Garnish with green chillies and coriander leaves.
- Serve *outengar maachor tenga* with plain rice.

Note: A delicacy to eat on a sunny day, it is normally served in an Assamese feast in the *outenga* season. If the above dish is cooked with *chital maach* (Notopterus) and served with steaming hot *joha chaul*, it is simply delicious.

Dhekia Aru Bilahir Tenga
Tomato and Dhekia Tenga

Ingredients

Rohu fish	:	8 pieces
Salt and turmeric powder	:	to rub on the fish pieces
Mustard oil	:	to fry the fish pieces + 1 tbsp
Sliced tomatoes	:	750 gms
Chopped *dhekia xaak*	:	50 gms
Mustard seeds	:	½ tsp
Turmeric powder	:	1 level tsp
Hot water	:	600 ml
Lime juice	:	2 tbsps
Salt and sugar	:	to taste
To garnish	:	green chillies and a piece of lemon

Method

§ Clean the fish. Rub it with salt and turmeric powder. Keep it aside for 5 minutes.

§ Fry the fish till half done. Keep the fried fish on a paper napkin to drain excess oil.

§ In a karai, heat fresh mustard oil. Splutter the mustard seeds it. Add the tomatoes, chopped *dhekia*, turmeric powder and salt.

§ Cook upon a low fire until the tomatoes become puree-like. Add hot water. Bring to boil and let it simmer for 10 minutes.

- § Add the fish and let it simmer till the fish pieces are soft. Add the lime juice and sugar. Stir well.
- § Garnish with chillies and a piece of lemon.
- § Serve hot *dhekia aru bilahir tenga* with rice.

Note: The aroma of lime relieves stress. During pregnancy, one should have lemon for better bone development of the child. The fresh rind of the lemon (*kaji nemu*) is good for digestion.

The regeneration frequency of the wild dhekia xaak is very high. Between the months of April and September, a fresh harvest can be made from the same lot within three to four days.

Kothal Gutir Lagot Maachor Tenga
Fish Tenga With Jackfruit Seeds

Ingredients

Rohu fish	:	8 pieces
Salt and turmeric powder	:	to rub on the fish
Mustard oil	:	to fry the fish pieces + 1tbsp
Jackfruit seeds	:	200 gms
Hot water	:	800 ml
Kharisa	:	2 tbsps
Turmeric powder	:	½ tsp
Mustard seeds	:	a pinch
Fresh red chillies	:	2
Lime juice	:	according to taste
Salt and sugar	:	to taste
To garnish	:	*maan dhania*

Method

§ Clean and wash the fish. Rub it with salt and turmeric powder.
§ Heat the mustard oil in a karai and fry the fish pieces till half done.
§ Wash the dried seeds of the jackfruit. Boil the seeds.
§ Remove the outer layer and also the inner red skin of the seeds with a sharp knife. Mash them.
§ Mix the hot water, salt, turmeric powder and *kharisa* with the mashed seeds.
§ Heat the fresh mustard oil in a karai. Splutter the mustard seeds in it and add the fresh red chillies. Add the jackfruit seed mixture.

- § Let it boil and simmer for 2 minutes. Sprinkle sugar and add the fish. Cover and let it simmer.
- § When the *tenga* thickens and the fish is soft, remove from the fire. Add the lime juice. Stir well.
- § Garnish with *maan dhania* and serve *kothal gutir lagot maachor tenga* along with steamed rice and green chillies.

Note: The fruit, flower, leaf, thorn and the roots of the lime tree of Assam have medicinal properties. It's a common practice among the Assamese people to make lime pickle only with salt because of its medicinal values. As the pickle matures, its medicinal properties increase.

Thekera Aru Alu Tenga
Potato Tenga with Cocum

Ingredients

Rohu fish	:	6 pieces
Salt and turmeric powder	:	to rub on the fish pieces
Mustard oil	:	for frying the fish pieces + 1 tbsp
Boiled and mashed potatoes	:	½ cup
Hot water	:	600 ml
Turmeric powder	:	½ level tsp
Fenugreek seeds	:	a pinch
Dry cocum*(thekera)*	:	6
Salt	:	to taste
To garnish	:	coriander leaves

Method

§ Soak the cocum in half a cup of warm water for half an hour. Mash the cocum with the fingertips and strain.
§ Clean and wash the fish. Rub it with salt and turmeric powder. Keep it covered for 5 minutes.
§ Heat the oil in a karai and fry the fish till half done. Keep the fried fish on a paper napkin to drain excess oil.
§ Mix the mashed potatoes with hot water. Add salt and turmeric powder to it.
§ Heat fresh mustard oil in a karai and add the fenugreek seeds. When the seeds turn red, add the hot potato mixture.

§ Let it boil. Cover and let it simmer for 5 minutes. Add the fish. Cook until the fish pieces are soft. Add the cocum juice. Stir well. Garnish with coriander leaves.
§ Serve *thekera aru alu tenga* with steamed *joha* rice and green chillies.

Note: *Thekera* (cocum) is widely used in Assam for its medicinal properties. It is used for all types of stomach ailments. Fresh squash made of *thekera* is often used as a cure for stomach ailments.

Narikolor Rosot Maach
Fish with Coconut Juice

Ingredients

Fish (*ari*)	:	1 kg (12 pieces)
Salt	:	to rub on the fish pieces
Mustard oil	:	for frying the fish pieces + 3 tbsps (for cooking)
Cardamom (green)	:	4
Cinnamon	:	1 inch long
Green chillies	:	3
Onions (chopped into rings)	:	2 large-sized
Coconut paste	:	1 tbsp
Coconut milk	:	180 ml
Raisins	:	50 gms
Hot water	:	200 ml
Sugar	:	½ level tsp
Salt	:	to taste
To garnish	:	coriander leaves green chillies

Method

§ Clean and wash the fish pieces. Rub the fish with salt and marinate for 5 minutes.
§ Fry the fish till half done. Drain excess oil on a paper towel.
§ Heat the fresh mustard oil. Add the cardamom, broken cinnamon sticks and green chillies and stir for a few seconds.

- § Add the onions. Fry till they are soft. Add the coconut paste with 1 tbsp of water and stir upon a low fire for about half a minute.
- § Add the coconut milk, raisins, hot water, salt and sugar. Let it boil.
- § Add the fish, cover and let it simmer upon a low fire until the fish pieces are soft.
- § Garnish with coriander leaves and green chillies.
- § Serve *narikolor rosot maach* with *chunga chaul*.

Note: When a roasted bamboo is split and the *chunga chaul* is taken out, a thin white layer of calcium covers the rice.

Paleng Xaakor Maachor Jhul
Fish Curry with Spinach

Ingredients

Fish (*sol*)	:	10 pieces
Salt and turmeric powder	:	to rub the fish pieces wtih
Mustard oil	:	for frying the fish pieces + 3 tbsps (for cooking)
Chopped spinach	:	250 gms
Potato (diced into ½ inch cube)	:	2 medium-sized
Shelled peas	:	½ cup
Panch phuron	:	½ level tsp
Sliced onions	:	1 medium-sized
Green chillies (optional)	:	2
Turmeric powder	:	1 level tsp
Hot water	:	800 ml
Crushed ginger	:	1 tbsp
Freshly ground pepper	:	1 level tsp
Salt	:	to taste

Method

§ Clean and wash the fish.
§ Rub the fish with salt and turmeric powder.
§ Heat the mustard oil and fry the fish until half done.
§ Heat the fresh mustard oil. Add the *panch phuron*. When it turns red, add the onions and fry them until soft, but not brown.
§ Add the chopped spinach, diced potatoes, peas, chillies, salt and turmeric powder. Stir for a minute and cover.

- Stir occasionally. When the potatoes are almost soft and dry, add hot water. Let it boil.
- Cover and let it simmer for about 10 minutes upon moderate fire.
- Add the fish pieces and crushed ginger.
- Let it simmer till the fish is soft.
- Add the pepper. Enjoy *paleng xaakor maachor jhul* on a cold winter night.

Note: Equal quantities of cumin seeds, mustard seeds, fenugreek seeds, coriander seeds and nigella are used to make *panch phuron*.

Variation – The above fish curry can also be made with spinach and cauliflower or spinach and radish. A few chopped fenugreek leaves can also be added to the spinach.

This curry made with spinach is a very popular dish in Assam during the winter season. The scientific name of the sol fish is Channa striatus.

Doi Maach
Curd Fish

Ingredients

Fish (boneless)	:	8 pieces
Salt	:	1 tsp
Turmeric powder	:	½ level tsp
Curd (whisked)	:	150 ml
Sugar	:	1 tsp
Mustard oil	:	3 tbsps
Nigella	:	a pinch
Green cardamom	:	4
Green chillies	:	2
Tomato sauce	:	2 tbsps
To garnish	:	sliced tomatoes mint leaves

Method

§ Clean and wash the fish.
§ Add salt, turmeric powder, curd and sugar to the fish. Mix well and marinate for 15 minutes.
§ Heat the mustard oil. Temper the nigella, cardamom and green chillies.
§ Add the fish to the curd mixture. Add the tomato sauce.
§ Cook over a slow fire. Turn the fish pieces slowly after 5 minutes.
§ Cook till the fish is tender and almost dry.
§ Garnish with sliced tomatoes and mint leaves and serve.
§ *Doi maach* can also be served chilled.

The fish used in the above recipe is known as kach and its scientific name is Silundia gangetica. It is a fish without scales.

Narasinghar Lagot Magur Maach
Cat Fish with Curry Leaves

Ingredients

Magur maach	:	2 (300 gms)
Salt and turmeric powder	:	to rub on the fish pieces
Mustard oil	:	for frying the fish pieces + 2 tbsps
Curry leaf paste	:	½ cup
Cumin seeds	:	a pinch
Bay leaves	:	2
Crushed garlic	:	2 tsps
Freshly ground pepper	:	½ tsp
Turmeric powder	:	½ level tsp
Salt	:	to taste
Warm water	:	300 ml

Method

- Cut the fish into pieces. Clean them. Rub the pieces with salt and turmeric powder. Marinate for 5 minutes.
- Heat the mustard oil and fry the fish pieces till half done.
- Heat the fresh mustard oil. Add the cumin seeds, bay leaves and crushed garlic, one by one.
- When the garlic changes colour, add the curry leaf paste, turmeric powder and salt.
- Stir upon a low fire for half a minute. Add the hot water and let it boil by increasing the heat.
- Add the fried fish. Cover and let it simmer for 6 minutes or until

the fish pieces are tender and the curry thickens.
§ Add the freshly ground pepper powder.
§ Serve hot *narasinghar lagot magur maach* with rice.

Note: This curry is given to a patient suffering from a cold and it also relieves body pain.

Mur Priya Aahar

My Favourite Dishes

Tel Phuit Khar

If you cross the river Luit to the northern side from Guwahati, it will take you about two and half hours to reach Nalbari. Whenever I think of Nalbari, one of the dishes that comes to my mind is *tel phuit khar*. It is a favourite breakfast dish of the local people of Nalbari. In Lower Assam, *kolakhar* is also known as *phuit khar*. If you mix mustard oil with the *kolakhar*, it is called *tel phuit khar* and is very easy to make.

Ingredients

Kolakhar	:	2 tbsps
Mustard oil	:	1 tbsp
Water	:	3 tbsps
Finely chopped onion	:	1 medium-sized
Chopped chillies	:	2
Salt	:	to taste

Method

§ Mix the *kolakhar*, mustard oil, water, finely chopped onion, chopped chillies and salt in a small bowl.
§ Serve *tel phuit khar* with *poita bhat* and baked potatoes.

Note: Enjoy *tel phuit khar* on a hot sunny day with *poita bhat* as breakfast. It will keep your body cool.

Sewali Phulor Khar
Coral Jasmine Khar

In autumn, the night air is filled with the sweet smell of *sewali phul*. The flower blooms at night and sheds dawn. These flowers are then collected on a cloth sheet which is often tied to the branches of the tree, or just spread on the ground. These flowers are palatable and are cooked, fresh or dried.

Ingredients

Dry *sewali phul*	:	½ cup
Broken rice (*khud chaul*)	:	½ cup
Water	:	600 ml
Fish head (rohu fish)	:	250 gms
Oil	:	for frying the fish head
Kolakhar	:	2 tbsps
Slit green chillies	:	3
Salt	:	to taste
Mustard oil	:	2 tbsps

Method

§ Clean the fish head. Cut the fish head into 4 pieces. Clean the pieces well.
§ Rub the fish pieces with salt and fry them till half done. Keep the pieces on a paper napkin to drain excess oil.
§ Clean and wash the *sewali phul* well.
§ Put the water, *khud chaul* and the flowers in a karai. Put the karai upon medium heat.

- When the water starts to boil, add the fried fish pieces. Reduce the heat to minimum.
- Cover and stir occasionally.
- When the *khud chaul is* almost done, add the green chillies, *kolakhar* and salt. Stir well.
- When the gravy thickens, remove the karai from the fire and add the fresh mustard oil.
- Mix it well and serve *sewali phulor khar* with plain rice as a first course for lunch.

The scientific name of sewali phul is Nyctanthes abortristis. It can be found in many places in India. Sewali phul is known as raat ki rani in Hindi.

Mosundari Aru Nohoru
Mosundari with Garlic

If I tell you that it takes only one minute to cook this herb, I am sure you will not believe me. So I think it is better if you try it yourself.

Ingredients

Mosundari xaak	:	200 gms
Mustard oil	:	2 tbsp
Garlic cloves	:	20-30
Salt	:	to taste

Method

§ Clean the *xaak* along with their tender stems.
§ Heat 1 tbsp of oil in a small heavy karai. Add garlic cloves and the *xaak*. Cover it.
§ After a minute, remove the karai from the fire. Add the salt and the remaining mustard oil. Mix well. Fresh chillies can be added as well.
§ Serve *mosundari aru nohoru* with plain hot rice.

Note: The scientific name of *mosundari* is Houttuynia cordata and is a very effective herb for curing severe dysentery. It is also proven to be a blood purifier.

The *durun xaak* (Leucas linifolia) is called chota halkusha in Hindi. If baked wrapped in a banana leaf, it increases the appetite and improves digestion. It is good for tonsillitis and if had as a curry made with ginger, garlic and fresh pepper, it is a good cure for colds.

Kothalguti Pitika
Mashed Jackfruit Seeds

If you want to enjoy simple food during hot summer days, what would be better than enjoying your rice and daal with *kothalguti pitika*.

Ingredients

Dried jackfruit seeds	:	25
Chopped green chillies	:	1 level tsp
Chopped coriander leaves	:	2 tsps
Mustard oil	:	1 tsp
Salt	:	to taste

Method

§ Clean the seeds. Cut 2-3 lines on each seed with a sharp knife.
§ Bake upon a slow charcoal fire till done. Clean them.
§ Mash it with the chopped chillies, coriander leaves, mustard oil and salt.
§ Enjoy *kothalguti pitika* with rice and daal.

Note: Jackfruit seeds can be baked in the oven by wrapping them in a banana leaf or in a silver foil. Potatoes and tomatoes are also baked similarly.

Koldil Bhaji
Spadix Fry

In Assam, the spadix (flower of the banana) of the banana named *aatheya* is normally eaten. But the spadix of any variety of banana can be eaten provided the bitter taste is removed by soaking the finely cut spadix in water mixed with salt and turmeric powder for about 6 hours. It is then crushed with the fingertips and washed and squeezed.

Ingredients

Koldil (banana flower)	:	1
Salt	:	1 level tsp
Turmeric powder	:	½ tsp
Mustard oil	:	5 tbsps
Bay leaves	:	2
Finely chopped onions	:	2 medium-sized
Potatoes (diced into ½ inch size)	:	2 medium-sized
Broken dry red chillies	:	2
Cinnamon (crushed)	:	(1 inch stick)
Cardamom (crushed)	:	4
Pure ghee	:	3 tsps
Salt	:	to taste

Method

§ Remove the outer layers of the *koldil* till you get the soft whitish layers.
§ Take some water in a large bowl. Add the salt and turmeric powder to it and cut the *koldil* finely.

- § Mash the finely chopped *koldil* with the fingertips. Squeeze out the water.
- § Heat the mustard oil in a wok or karai. Add the bay leaves.
- § When the bay leaves change colour, add the onions. Stir the onions upon medium heat.
- § When the onions are slightly brown, add the diced potatoes. Stir for a while.
- § Add the chillies, *koldil* and sprinkle the salt. Stir upon medium heat for a minute.
- § Sprinkle crushed cinnamon and cardamom. Cover and reduce the heat to minimum. Stir occasionally.
- § When the potatoes are soft, add 2 tsps of pure ghee. Increase the heat. Stir continuously for a minute.
- § Add the remaining ghee. Stir well.
- § Remove the *koldil bhaji* from the fire and serve.
- § *Koldil bhaji* is delicious if made with pigeon meat or chicken.

Note: The *aatheya* spadix has medicinal values. Tuberculosis patients should eat spadix fry once a day for 8-10 days. It provides relief from headaches if the spadix is made with freshly ground pepper. It is good for diabetes, epilepsy, gonorrhea etc.

Kosu Tenga
Sour Colocasia

Kosu tenga is one of the favourite recipes of the people of this part of India. In the rural areas, one can get ample quantities of colocasia without much effort. Since my childhood I have noticed that people's hair gray very late in the rural areas. One of the reasons may be that the unopened long, tender leaf of the colocasia is believed to delay the graying of hair.

Ingredients

Kosur thur (colocasia leaves with tender stems)	:	500 gms
Mustard oil	:	2 tbsps
Mustard seeds	:	½ level tsp
Crushed garlic	:	1 tbsp
Dry red chillies	:	3
Cherry tomatoes	:	200 gms
Turmeric powder	:	½ tsp
Mustard seed paste	:	1 tbsp
Warm water	:	500 ml
Freshly ground pepper	:	2 tsps
Lime juice	:	2-3 tbsps
Salt	:	to taste
To garnish	:	cherry tomatoes

Method

§ Pick the colocasia leaves on a sunny day. Clean, wash and chop coarsely.

- § Boil the leaves for 20 minutes with enough water and then drain the water. Mash them with a spoon.
- § Heat the mustard oil. Splutter the mustard seeds in it and add the crushed garlic and red chillies.
- § When the garlic turns brown, add the cherry tomatoes, colocasia leaves, turmeric powder and salt.
- § Stir upon medium heat for 2 minutes. Add the mustard seed paste and water.
- § Cover and let it simmer till the gravy thickens. Stir occasionally.
- § Add the lime juice, pepper and cover. Remove from the fire after half a minute.
- § Garnish it with cherry tomatoes.
- § Serve *kosu tenga* with plain rice. Some small fried fish can be added as well.

Maachor Petu Bhoja
Fried Fish Guts

Fish has plenty to offer. You must only know how to enjoy it. *Maachor petu bhoja* is one of the most popular dishes of Assamese cuisine. It is a dish which is had at the beginning of a meal with boiled rice.

One of the most delicious parts of the fish is the fish oil present in the guts. The portion of the fat attached to the intestine should be cleaned properly. Care should be also taken so that the gall bladder attached to the liver is not punctured. Otherwise this will make the fat bitter.

Ingredients

Cooked rice	:	200 gms
Fish guts	:	75 gms
Mustard oil	:	2 tbsps
Sliced onions	:	2 medium-sized
Dry red chillies	:	2
Turmeric powder	:	½ level tsp
Salt	:	to taste

Method

§ Clean and wash the fish guts.
§ Heat the mustard oil in a karai. Add the sliced onions and the red chillies.
§ Stir till the onions are soft.

- § Add the fish guts and cook upon medium heat for about 5 minutes. Stir continuously.
- § Add the turmeric powder, salt and the cooked rice.
- § Cook for another 2 minutes.
- § Serve hot *maachor petu bhoja* with plain j*oha* rice.

Note: Fish guts can be enjoyed as kababs too. Mix the fish guts with rice powder, finely chopped onions, green chillies, chopped coriander leaves, turmeric powder and salt. Make a few balls, flatten the balls and deep fry till golden brown. They can be served as starters.

Fish guts contains omega 3 fatty acid which reduces the risk of a heart attack. Omega 3 also protects one against certain types of cancer.

Kharisar Tenga
Fermented Bamboo Shoot Tenga

One of the main Assamese vegetarian dishes is *tenga* made with *bor*. *Kharisar tenga* is one of these.

Ingredients

Dhekia	:	100 gms
Kharisa	:	3 tbsps
Boiled potatoes	:	2 medium-sized
Red lentil	:	50 gms
Mustard oil	:	100 ml
Fenugreek seeds	:	a pinch
Boiling water	:	1 litre
Broken green chillies	:	3
Turmeric powder	:	⅓ tsp
Salt	:	to taste

Method

§ Soak the lentil for 2 hours. Grind to a smooth paste.
§ Chop the *dhekia*. Mash the boiled potatoes.
§ Sprinkle salt to the lentil batter. Mix well.
§ Heat the mustard oil in a karai. Make small pakoras and fry till half done, and put them on a paper napkin to soak excess oil.
§ In 2 tbsps of hot oil, add the fenugreek seeds. When they turn red, add the chopped *dhekia*.
§ Stir for 2 minutes upon medium heat.

- § Add boiling water, *kharisa*, salt and turmeric powder to the mashed potatoes. Mix well.
- § Pour the hot potato mixture into the karai. Increase the heat, cover and cook for about 7 minutes.
- § Add the half-fried *bors*. Cover and let it simmer till the *bors* are soft.
- § Add the broken green chillies and remove from the fire.
- § Enjoy *kharisar tenga* with rice, green chillies and a piece of lemon.

Note: *Dhekia* is a species of fern widely grown in Assam. It is one of the cheapest vegetables with the best nutritive values. The crude protein obtained from *dhekia* is much more than the protein of any type of meat. The tender leaves of *dhekia* contains 33.27 per cent of protein.

Pura Goroi Maachor Pitika
Barbequed Fish

A mud water small fish named *goroi* whose scientific name is *Ophioce phalus punctatus* is delicious if barbequed as in this recipe.

Ingredients

Goroi fish	:	500 gms
Bamboo spikes	:	8
Mustard oil	:	2 tbsps
Kharisa (fermented bamboo shoot)	:	2 tbsps
Chopped onions	:	2 medium-sized
Chopped coriander leaves	:	one small bunch
Chopped chillies	:	2
Salt	:	to taste

Method

§ Clean the fish and remove the intestines. Wash it well.
§ Take the whole *goroi* fish and spear each one vertically on round and thin bamboo spikes.
§ Stick the bamboo spikes at a distance of about 6 inches from the fire till done.
§ Rotate the spike and roast the other side of the fish as well.
§ Once the fish cools, remove the bones.
§ Mix the fish with mustard oil, *kharisa*, chopped onions, coriander leaves, chopped green chillies and salt.
§ Serve *pura goroi maachor pitika* as a first course with rice and daal.

Adar Jhul
Ginger Curry

Barpeta is situated on the northern bank of the river Brahmaputra. It's about a three hour drive from Guwahati. The people of Barpeta have been retaining their rich culture. The famous Vaishnavite temple Kirtan Ghar is in Barpeta and is it the soul of the people there. One of the popular cuisines of Barpeta is the following curry.

Ingredients

Fish	:	6 pieces
Salt and turmeric powder	:	to rub the fish pieces
Mustard oil	:	to fry the fish pieces
Mustard oil	:	2 tbsps
Nigella	:	a pinch
Ginger	:	75 gms
Turmeric powder	:	½ level tsp
Green chillies	:	3
Hot water	:	300 ml
Maan dhania (chopped)	:	1 tbsp
Salt	:	to taste

Method

§ Clean and wash the fish.
§ Rub the fish with salt and turmeric and fry them till half done.
§ Crush the ginger and take out the juice.
§ Heat the fresh mustard oil in a karai. Add the nigella.

- § Add the ginger juice, turmeric powder and chillies. Also add hot water and salt.
- § When the curry starts to boil, add the fish pieces and cover.
- § Let it simmer for about 10 minutes or till the fish pieces are almost done. Add *maan dhania* and cover for a minute. Remove the karai from the fire.
- § Serve hot *adar jhul* with rice.

Note: *Maan dhania* (Eryngium) is a kind of pot herb which smells like the coriander leaf. It is also known as *naga dhania*. If unavailble, use coriander leaves.

Magur Maach Aru Bhedailotar Jhul
Cat Fish Curry with King Tonic

King tonic is known as *bhedailota* in Assam. Its fresh leaves have a very strong smell. In Assam, it is often eaten as a curry prepared with fresh fish. King tonic curry is given to a mother after a pregnancy and is prepared with cat fish and pepper.

Ingredients

Cat fish	:	6 pieces
Tender king tonic leaves	:	75 gms
Mustard oil	:	2 tbsps
Garlic cloves	:	10
Black pepper (whole)	:	15
Warm water	:	300 ml
Turmeric powder	:	a pinch
Salt and pepper	:	to taste
To garnish	:	garlic cloves

Method

§ Clean the fish.
§ Make a paste of the king tonic leaves.
§ Heat the oil in a karai. Add garlic cloves and pepper and stir.
§ When the garlic cloves are brown, add the king tonic paste, the raw fish pieces, turmeric powder, freshly ground pepper and salt.
§ Stir for a while and add hot water.
§ Cover and let it simmer till the fish is soft and done.

§ Garnish it with garlic cloves and serve *magur maach aru bhedailotar jhul* with hot *joha* rice.

Note: King tonic increases the appetite and is good for allergy, paralysis and rheumatism. Its juice is good for stomach ailments like diarrhoea.

During Bohag and Magh Bihu, a special curry of king tonic and different varieties of edible colacosia leaves, ginger, garlic and pepper with fresh fish is enjoyed in parts of Assam.

Xaakor Jhul
Herbs Curry

Sivasagar, 369 kms east of Guwahati is better known for its historic relics, temples and tanks. The famous Borpukhuri, a massive man-made tank, covers an area of 129 acres. The level of water in the tank is always above the ground level of Sivasagar town. However, the biggest man-made tank Joysagar covering an area of 318 acres (including its four banks) is also in the Sivasagar district. Many people of this district harness fish in small ponds in their backyard.

So if you get a chance of having lunch at local resident's place in Sivasagar, you may be served this fresh fish curry for lunch.

Ingredients

Mixed herbs	:	150 gms
Fish pieces (rohu)	:	6
Mustard oil	:	2 tbsps
Garlic cloves	:	25
Chopped ginger	:	1 inch piece
Turmeric powder	:	a pinch
Salt	:	to taste
Water	:	300 ml
Rice powder	:	1 tsp
To garnish	:	crushed pepper

Method

§ Clean and wash the herbs. Chop then.

- § Clean and wash the fish.
- § In a small pressure cooker, heat the mustard oil. Sauté the garlic cloves.
- § When the cloves are slightly brown add the *xaak*, chopped ginger, turmeric powder and the salt. Also add the raw fish pieces.
- § Sauté for a minute. Mix the rice powder with the water and add it to the *xaak*.
- § Close the pressure cooker and bring it to full pressure.
- § Reduce the heat and remove the pressure cooker from the fire after 5 minutes.
- § When the cooker cools down, open the cover. Sprinkle the crushed pepper.
- § Serve hot *xaakor jhul* with *joha* rice.

Suklatir Jhul
Suklati Curry

When my first child was born, my husband and I were posted in Duliajan. Duliajan is a place in the eastern part of Assam. Herbs play a very important role in its day-to-day life. My *jethai* (aunt) would bring home-cooked meals for me to the hospital. One day she bought this special dish *suklatir jhul* which is supposed to hasten the healing process. *Suklati* is not available in plenty but can be easily grown.

Ingredients

Suklati xaak	: 100 gms
Small fish	: 200 gms
Salt and turmeric powder	: to rub the fish with
Mustard oil	: to fry the small fish + 1 tbsp (for the curry)
Fenugreek seeds	: a pinch
Garlic cloves	: 8
Hot water	: 350 ml
Turmeric powder	: ⅓ level tsp
Salt	: to taste
Freshly ground pepper	: a pinch

Method

§ Clean and wash the small fish. Rub the fish with salt and turmeric powder.
§ Clean the herbs. Crush them and take out the juice.

Jyoti Das

- § Heat oil in a karai. Fry the fish and keep it on a paper napkin to soak excess oil.
- § Heat the fresh mustard oil in a karai. Add the fenugreek seeds and garlic cloves.
- § When the seeds turn red, add the *suklati* juice and hot water. Sprinkle the salt and turmeric powder.
- § Cover and let it simmer for 5 minutes.
- § Add the fried fish and let it simmer for 5-7 minutes or until the fish is soft.
- § Remove the curry from the fire. Sprinkle pepper powder over it.
- § Serve hot *suklatir jhul* with hot rice.

Thekerar Maachor Tenga
Fish Tenga with Cocum

In some places like Tihu of the Nalbari district, *thekerar maachor tenga* is a very popular dish. Vegetables or spices are not used for this dish. Rice paste is used as a thickening agent. There is a popular saying, *'Anjat boton nomabor jaton'* which means 'as one adds the rice paste to the curry, it is almost done'.

Ingredients

Fresh small fish	:	8 (500 gms)
Salt and turmeric powder	:	to rub the fish with
Rice	:	2 tsps
Thekera (cocum)	:	6 pieces
Warm water	:	100 ml
Mustard oil	:	to fry the fish + 1 tbsp (to make the *tenga*)
Fenugreek seeds	:	a pinch
Hot water	:	600 ml
Turmeric powder	:	½ level tsp
Salt	:	to taste

Method

§ Clean and wash the fish. Rub it with turmeric powder and salt and keep it covered for 5 minutes.
§ Soak the rice for 10 minutes and make a smooth paste.
§ Soak the dry *thekera* in 100 ml of warm water for half an hour. Mash the softened *thekera* with the fingers.

- § Heat the oil in a frying pan and fry the fish till half done. Keep the fish on a paper napkin to soak excess oil.
- § In a karai, heat 1 tbsp of fresh mustard oil. Add the fenugreek seeds to it. When the seeds turn red, add the *thekera* along with the water. Also add the hot water.
- § Sprinkle the turmeric powder and salt and let it cook for 5 minutes.
- § Add the fried fish and cover. Let it simmer for 5 minutes.
- § Add a little water to the rice paste and add it to the curry.
- § Stir carefully. After a minute, remove the sour curry from the fire.
- § Serve *thekerar maachor tenga* with rice and fresh green chillies.

Sarioh Xaakor Lagot Gahori Manxo
Pork with Mustard Leaves

During the cold season when mustard leaves are plenty in the kitchen garden, the tender leaves are used to make *sarioh xaakar lagot gahori manxo*. I first tasted it at a picnic party on the banks of Dehing river of Dibrugarh district. It was delicious that I can distinctly remember the taste. It is normally served with *laopani (saaj)*

Ingredients

Pork (cut into serving portions)	:	1 kg
Mustard leaves (*sarioh xaak*)	:	350 gms
Slit green chillies	:	6
Water	:	350 ml
Mustard oil	:	6 tbsps
Sliced onions	:	4 medium-sized
Crushed garlic	:	1 tbsp
Salt and pepper	:	to taste

Method

§ Wash the pork and drain excess water.
§ Clean the mustard leaves and tear them with your hands.
§ Boil the pork with the slit green chillies and water in a pressure cooker for ten minutes upon medium heat. Let it cool.
§ Open the pressure cooker and put it upon the fire till the meat is dry. Stir occasionally.
§ Heat the mustard oil in a pan. Add the sliced onions and crushed garlic and stir upon medium heat.

Jyoti Das

§ When the onions are soft, add the mustard leaves, pork and sprinkle some salt.
§ When the mustard leaves disintegrate and mix with the meat, increase the heat and stir for a minute.
§ Sprinkle the freshly ground pepper and serve *sarioh xaakor lagot gahori manxo* as an appetiser with alcoholic beverages.

Note: Mustard seeds are also known as *behor*.

Mur Maar Kukurar Vyanjan
My Mother's Chicken Recipe

This is a chicken dish which my mother often makes whenever I visit her. It is also one of her grandchildren's favourites.

Ingredients

Two tender country chickens	:	1 ½ kg
Ginger	:	100 gms
Refined oil	:	100 gms
Bay leaves	:	4
Chopped onions	:	8 medium-sized
Salt and sugar	:	according to taste.

Method

- Clean and cut the chicken into desired pieces.
- Crush the ginger and take out the juice.
- Heat the oil in a karai and add bay leaves and half of the chopped onions. Stir upon medium heat till the onions are soft, but not brown.
- Add the chicken. Sprinkle the salt and sugar and stir for a minute.
- Reduce the heat to minimum and cover. When the chicken pieces are half done, add the remaining chopped onions and the ginger juice.
- Stir for a few seconds. Cover it and let it simmer in its own juices till the chicken pieces are tender.
- Remove the cover. Stir for about a minute.
- *Mur maar kukurar vyanjan* is delicious with hot parathas.

Kukurar Suruha
Assamese Chicken Soup

During our childhood days, whenever we were sick, our mother used to make a chicken soup which was not only tasty but which also helped us to regain our strength.

Ingredients

Tender country chicken	:	500 gms
Bay leaf	:	1
Green cardamom (crushed)	:	1
Salt	:	to taste

Method

- § Clean the chicken and cut it into pieces.
- § Steam the chicken pieces adding the bay leaf and the crushed green cardamom in a pressure cooker for 10 minutes.
- § When the cooker cools slightly, open it and strain the chicken juice.
- § Add salt to taste.
- § Serve hot *kukurar suruha* with a little pepper.

Mitha Ahar

Dessert

After a midday meal, especially in the summers, a dessert is a must and the meal is completed with curd, eaten with a little rice and jaggery or simply sweetened with jaggery.

Fresh fruit like mangoes, pineapples or jackfruit are also relished after lunch or dinner.

Payas is one of the most common sweet dishes found in every household. Not only is it served as a dessert, but also served to a guest. *Payas* is also offered as a *prasad* to the deity. Though rice *payas* is the most common *payas*, it is also made with rice powder, carrots, pumpkin, papaya, semolina etc.

Certain sweet dishes like custard, caramel pudding etc are also popular in Assam. A few deserts which I serve along with Assamese food are also included in the following section.

Panilaor Payas
Bottlegourd Payas

Ingredients

Grated bottlegourd	:	2 cups
Water	:	350 ml
Milk	:	2 litres
Bay leaves	:	3
Sugar	:	5 tbsps
Pistachio (chopped)	:	8
Cashewnuts (chopped)	:	10
Raisins	:	20
Green cardamom (crushed)	:	4

Method

§ Boil the bottlegourd in 350 ml of water for 2 minutes. Drain the water. When it cools, squeeze out the water from the bottlegourd.
§ Boil the milk and reduce it to half.
§ Add the bottlegourd, bay leaves and cook for 20 minutes upon moderate heat. Stir occasionally.
§ Add the sugar, pistachio, raisins, cashewnuts and cook till done.
§ Sprinkle the crushed cardamom and cover it.
§ Serve chilled *panilaor payas*.

Note: Cashewnut is a rich source of protein.

Chaulor Payas
Rice Payas

Ingredients

Milk	:	1 litre
Joha rice	:	30 gms
Pure ghee	:	2 tbsps
Bay leaves	:	2
Sugar	:	100 gms
Raisins	:	25-30
Cardamom (crushed)	:	6

Method

§ Wash the rice and drain the excess water.
§ Heat a pan. Add ghee and fry the rice till it turns a light golden in colour.
§ Boil the milk for about 5 minutes. Add the rice and the bay leaves.
§ When the rice is cooked, add the sugar and raisins.
§ Keep stirring. When the *payas* thickens, remove from the fire.
§ Sprinkle the cardamom. Stir.
§ Serve chilled *chaulor payas*.

Note: Raisins are a good source of natural sugar and fibre.

Pithagurir Payas
Rice Powder Payas

Ingredients

Milk	:	1½ litre
Sugar	:	100 gms
Rice powder	:	110 gms
Vanilla essence	:	1 tsp
To garnish	:	a tender lemon leaf

Method

- Keep 300 ml of milk aside.
- Boil the remaining milk in a pan and reduce it to about 750 ml upon low heat and stir occasionally.
- Mix the rice powder with 300 ml of milk and add it to the milk.
- Stir continuously so that no lumps are formed.
- Add the sugar and stir.
- Add more milk if necessary.
- Keep stirring till the *payas* thickens. Remove from the fire.
- Add the vanilla essence. Mix well and cover it.
- Chill the *pithagurir payas* for 4-5 hours. Garnish with a lemon leaf and serve.

Note: Dry fried *pithaguri* (rice powder) is eaten with black tea and jaggery as *jalpan* (a light repast).

Alur Pudding
Potato Pudding

Ingredients

Milk	:	400 ml
Maida	:	35 gms
Boiled and mashed potatoes	:	½ cup
Sugar	:	100 gms
Eggs (beaten)	:	3
Butter	:	50 gms
Vanilla essence	:	½ tsp
Cream (whipped)	:	3 tbsps

Method

§ Mix the milk, maida and boiled mashed potatoes well. Add the sugar.
§ Cook upon slow fire and stir for about 7 minutes.
§ Let it cool. Add the beaten eggs, vanilla essence and butter. Mix well.
§ Pour it into a greased bowl and bake in moderate heat in an oven for one hour or until done.
§ Garnish *alur* pudding with whipped cream and serve it chilled.

Note: Cream and soft rice is an authentic and well-loved *jalpan* (a light repast) of the Assamese people.

Bhator Payas
Chilled Rice Pudding

Ingredients

Cooked rice	:	70 gms
Milk	:	750 ml
Butter	:	30 ml
Bay leaves	:	2
Sugar	:	75 gms
To garnish	:	grated lemon rind

Method

- Boil the milk in a heavy pan. Reduce the heat and let it simmer till the milk reduces to 500 ml.
- In another heavy-bottomed pan, heat the butter and add the bay leaves and rice. Stir for a minute.
- Add the milk and sugar. Let it simmer upon low heat till the milk is almost dry.
- Remove the pan from the fire and chill the *payas* for a few hours.
- Garnish *bhator payas* with green lemon rind.
- Serve in small bowls.

Note: *Sandahguri*, a coarse powder of parched rice is another *jalpan* relished with black tea and jaggery or with milk and jaggery.

Sewair Kheer
Vermicelli Kheer

Ingredients

Sewai (vermicelli)	:	75 gms
Pure ghee	:	1 tbsp
Cardamom	:	2
Milk	:	600 ml
Raisins	:	20 gms
Sugar	:	75 gms
Orange rind	:	½ tsp
Condensed milk	:	3 tbsps

Method

§ Heat pure ghee in a saucepan. Add the cardamom. Fry for a few seconds.
§ Add the vermicelli and fry. Stir continuously till the vermicelli is golden brown in colour.
§ Add the milk and let it boil. Add the raisins, sugar and the orange rind.
§ Leave it upon low heat for 10 minutes or till done.
§ Add the condensed milk. Stir well.
§ Serve warm or chilled *sewair kheer*.

Cornflouror Mitha Ahar
Cornflour Pudding

Ingredients

Amulspray powder	:	3 cups
Water	:	850 ml
Cocoa powder	:	2 tbsps
Hot water	:	100 ml
Cornflour	:	3 tbsps
Sugar	:	140 gms
Vanilla essence	:	1 tsp
Cream	:	100 ml
To garnish	:	grated chocolate

Method

§ Mix the milk powder with 750 ml of water.
§ Mix the cocoa powder with 100 ml of hot water and add it to the milk.
§ Mix the cornflour with the remaining 100 ml of water.
§ Heat the milk in a pan. When it starts to boil, reduce the heat.
§ Add the cornflour mixture. Stir continuously so that no lumps are formed. Add the sugar and stir for two minutes.
§ When done, remove from the fire. Add the vanilla essence and cream and mix well.
§ Let it cool and cover it so that no layer is formed. Chill for 4-5 hours.
§ Garnish *cornflouror mitha ahar* with grated chocolate and serve.

Vanilla Custard

Ingredients

Eggs	:	4
Milk	:	400 ml
Custard powder	:	1 tbsp
Cream	:	100 ml
Sugar	:	75 gms
Vanilla essence	:	1 tsp

Method

- Separate the egg yolks and beat them well. Keep the egg whites aside for some other use.
- Mix the custard powder in 50 ml of milk.
- In a heavy-bottomed pan, mix the remaining milk, egg yolks and cream.
- Heat the pan upon a low flame. Stir the milk mixture and add the sugar.
- When the milk is about to boil, add the custard and milk mixture and stir continuously.
- When the custard thickens, add the vanilla essence. Stir well and remove it from the fire.
- Stir for a few more minutes. Cover and let it cool so that no layer is formed.
- Chill and serve vanilla custard.

Caramel Pudding

Ingredients

Duck eggs	:	8
Amulspray powder milk	:	300 gms
Water	:	300 ml
Sugar	:	250 gms
Vanilla essence	:	1½ tsps

To caramelise:

Refined oil or butter	:	1 tbsp
Sugar	:	2 tsps

Method

§ Beat the eggs lightly. Put the beaten eggs, milk powder, water, sugar and essence in a mixie and blend.
§ Put a greased borosil bowl upon a low fire. Add the oil or butter.
§ When the oil starts to get warm, add the sugar.
§ Stir continuously with a thin wooden spoon until the sugar is deep brown in colour. Spread the caramelised sugar.
§ Remove the bowl from the fire. Set it aside for a few seconds in a warm place.
§ Pour the egg mixture into the caramelised sugar in the borosil bowl. Steam for 45 minutes or until done.
§ Push a sharp knife into the pudding. If the knife comes out clean, the pudding is done.

§ Overturn it on a plate, when slightly cool,
§ Serve chilled caramel pudding.

Note: I prefer to use duck eggs to make the caramel pudding. They give a lovely colour to the pudding as the yolks are yellowish orange in colour. I also use thick buffalo milk instead of powder milk. The use of lemon and orange rind is very common in Assam while making this pudding.

Rongalao Aru Paneeror Mitha Ahar

Pumpkin Cheese Cake

Ingredients

Thin Arrowroot biscuits	:	1 medium-sized packet
Butter	:	60 gms
Pumpkin (diced)	:	250 gms
Green cardamom (crushed)	:	6
Eggs	:	4
Sugar	:	150 gms
Paneer	:	250 gms
Powder milk	:	100 gms
Milk	:	200 ml
Nutmeg powder	:	½ level tsp

Method

§ Melt the butter in a pan. Break the biscuits and fry for a minute upon a low fire.
§ Powder the biscuits. Press it to the base and the sides of a baking bowl.
§ Steam the pumpkin with the crushed cardamom. Drain the water from the pumpkin.
§ When the pumpkin cools, put it into a mixie and blend till smooth.
§ Add the eggs, sugar, paneer, powder milk, milk, nutmeg powder and blend till the mixture is smooth.

- § Pour it into the prepared baking bowl and bake in a preheated oven at 180°C for 40 minutes or till done.
- § Check by inserting a sharp knife into the pumpkin cheese cake. It the knife comes out clean, the pudding is done.
- § Chill and serve *rongalao aru paneeror mitha ahar* with cream.

Note: The water soluble Vitamin C present in pumpkins is preserved if the pumpkin is steamed.

Norabogorir Rosot Norabogori
Delicious Peaches in Peach Syrup

Ingredients

Peach syrup	:	200 ml
Peaches	:	4
Cream	:	½ level tbsp

For the peach syrup:

Peaches	:	10
Sugar	:	250 gms
Water	:	350 ml

Method

§ Peel the peaches and cut them into pieces.
§ Put the peaches, sugar and water in a saucepan.
§ Cook upon medium heat for about 6-7 minutes. Let it cool and strain. The peach syrup is ready.
§ Peel the four peaches and keep them whole.
§ Heat the peach syrup in a small pan. When hot, add the whole peaches. Cover and cook for 2 minutes. Stir occasionally.
§ Remove the pan from the fire. Add the cream.
§ Serve chilled *norabogorir rosot norabogori*.

Note: The local peaches of Assam are sweet and tangy. The centre of the peach is deep red in colour.

Strawberry and Cream

Ingredients

Strawberries	:	20
Eggs	:	2
Fresh cream	:	200 ml
Milk	:	100 ml
Sugar (powdered)	:	75 gms
Lemon juice	:	1 tbsp
Grated lemon rind	:	1 level tsp

Method

- Separate the egg white and beat it in a dry bowl with a little powdered sugar till stiff. Keep the yolks aside for some other use.
- Whip the cream well. Add the powdered sugar and milk, a little at a time and keep whipping it till all the sugar and milk is absorbed.
- Add the lemon juice and lemon rind and mix well.
- Fold in the beaten egg whites.
- Divide the cream into 6 small pudding bowls and put it in the refrigerator.
- Just before serving it, garnish the pudding bowls with sliced strawberries and enjoy strawberry and cream.

Note: Strawberries are grown in some places in Assam.

Rongalaor Souffle
Pumpkin Souffle

Ingredients

Pumpkin	:	300 gms
Powder milk	:	150 gms
Milk	:	500 ml
Sugar	:	150 gms
Gelatin	:	3 tsps
Hot water	:	150 ml
Fresh cream	:	90 ml
Eggs	:	4
Orange juice	:	90 ml
Finely cut orange rind	:	1 tsp
To garnish	:	3 orange carpals

Method

§ Peel the pumpkin. Clean, wash and grate the pumpkin.
§ Mix the powder milk with the milk and pour it into a saucepan.
§ Put the saucepan upon a medium fire and add the grated pumpkin. Stir and add sugar.
§ After 7 minutes, remove the saucepan from the fire. Let it cool.
§ Mix the gelatin with the hot water and mix it with the pumpkin mixture.
§ Beat the cream. Add the cream to the pumpkin mixture and mix well.

§ Separate the egg whites. Keep the yolks aside for later use. Beat the egg whites till stiff.
§ Fold in the egg whites and also add the orange juice and orange peels to the pumpkin mixture.
§ Chill for 4 hours. Garnish it with orange carpals and serve *rongalaor* souffle with cream.

Phalor Lagot Cream
Fruit and Cream

Ingredients

Mangoes	:	2 medium-sized
Peaches	:	4
Lichis	:	10
Rose apple (white *jamun*)	:	4
Fresh cream	:	to lace the fruits
To garnish	:	grated lemon rind

Method

§ Peel the mangoes and peaches. Make pieces of desired size.
§ Peel the lichis. Clean the rose apples and slit them.
§ Arrange the fruits on a serving plate.
§ Chill for an hour.
§ Whip the cream and lace the fruits with the fresh cream.
§ Sprinkle lemon rind and serve immediately.
§ Enjoy *phalor lagot cream* as the dessert to complete an Assamese meal.

Assam is considered to be one of the most probable original homes of mangoes.

Baanhor Chungar Pudding
Bamboo Hollow Pudding

Ingredients

Semolina	:	1 cup
Milk	:	275 ml
Eggs	:	2
Sugar	:	175 gms
Cocoa powder	:	$1/3$ cup
Bamboo hollows	:	2
Banana leaves (small)	:	2
To garnish	:	crushed cashewnuts honey – 1 tbsp

Method

§ Soak the semolina in 200 ml of milk for an hour. Beat the eggs.
§ Heat the remaining 75 ml of milk and mix in the cocoa powder. Let it cool.
§ Blend the semolina, milk, beaten eggs, cocoa powder mixture and sugar in a blender.
§ Clean the bamboo hollows and hold the banana leaves over a low fire to make them pliable.
§ Fill the bamboo hollows with the semolina mixture leaving a two inch empty space at the top. Close the mouths of the hollows with banana leaves so that it becomes air tight.
§ Heat the bamboo hollows directly over a slow charcoal fire for about 20-25 minutes or till done.

- § Split the bamboo hollows with a sharp knife and take out the pudding. Cut out into round pieces.
- § Garnish with crushed cashewnuts and honey.
- § Serve *baanhor chungar* pudding chilled. It can be served in bamboo hollows too.

Note: The above pudding can be steamed as well.

Amitar Kheer
Papaya Kheer

Ingredients

Half-ripened papaya (diced)	:	250 gms
Milk	:	2 litres
Butter	:	1 tbsp
Bay leaves	:	2
Rice powder	:	1 tbsp
Sugar	:	80 gms
Vanilla essence	:	1 tsp

Method

§ Keep a cup of milk aside and put the remaining milk in a pan.
§ Boil the milk and reduce the heat. Reduce the milk to half.
§ Heat the butter in a pan. Add the bay leaves and stir for about 10 seconds. Add the diced papaya and stir for awhile.
§ Add warm milk and keep stirring occasionally for about 15 minutes or till the papaya is soft.
§ Mix the rice powder with the cup of milk and gradually add it to the pan. Stir continuously to avoid the formation of lumps.
§ Add the sugar and vanilla essence. Stir for another 2 minutes.
§ Remove the pan from the fire.
§ Chill and serve *amitar kheer*.

Komal Chaulor Payas
Soft Rice Payas

Ingredients

Milk	:	1½ litres
Soft rice (*komal chaul*)	:	60 gms
Refined oil	:	1 tbsp
Sugar	:	1 level tsp
Bay leaves	:	2
Raisins	:	25 gms
Jaggery	:	100 gms
Vanilla essence	:	1 tsp

Method

§ Boil the milk in a saucepan. Let it simmer and reduce the milk to half.
§ Soak the soft rice for an hour and drain the water.
§ Heat the oil in a pan. Caramelise the sugar. Add the bay leaves.
§ Add the soft rice and stir upon medium heat till brown.
§ Add the milk and stir. Keep the fire to a minimum.
§ After 8 minutes, add the raisins, jaggery and the vanilla essence.
§ When the payas thickens, remove it from the fire.
§ Chill *komal chaulor payas* and serve it as a dessert.

Note: *Komal chaul* is made from sticky rice paddy.

Lutharir Lagot Norabogori
Peaches and Rice Powder Pudding

Ingredients

For the peach syrup:
Peaches	:	10
Sugar	:	150 gms
Water	:	200 ml

For the pudding:
Peaches	:	6
Rice powder	:	5 tsps
Milk	:	350 ml
Sugar	:	50 gms
Cream (beaten)	:	50 ml

Method

§ Peel and slice the peaches to make the peach syrup.
§ In a heavy-bottomed pan, put the sliced peaches, sugar and water and cook upon medium heat. Stir continuously.
§ After 6-7 minutes, remove the pan from the fire and strain the peach syrup.
§ Peel the 6 peaches. Divide each peach into two equal parts. Put the 12 pieces in a pan and cook it in the peach syrup on a low fire for 2 minutes.
§ Remove the pan from the fire and let it cool.

- Mix the rice powder with milk and sugar in a saucepan. Put the saucepan on a low fire and keep stirring.
- When the rice pudding thickens, remove it from the fire. Add the beaten cream and keep stirring for 5 minutes.
- Pour the *luthari pudding* on a plate.
- Garnish it with the pieces of peach and pour the syrup over the them.
- Chill and serve.

Xaak and Saatxaaki

If you know how and where to look, you can find God everywhere. It is no different when it comes to finding *xaak*. By the creek, near the river bed, amongst the weeds, in the jungle, in the wet lands and more often than not in an Assamese backyard. So all you need to find *xaak*, is to have an eye for it. There are more than three thousand different varieties of *xaak* found in Assam. You can fry them, make fritters out of them, cook delicious fish with *xaak* and lots more. I believe that one can use them in almost any dish. One of my hobbies is to look for different varieties of *xaak*.

Xaak forms an indispensable part of Assamese cuisine. The *xaak* used may be bitter, sour, sweet or even astringent. *Xaak* has various preventive and curative medicinal properties. I remember my mother giving me a greenish curry to have, apparently made from ground *xaak* and roots, whenever I had any stomach ailment or was suffering from a cold. It did wonders within a short time. I named it *bhogobanor jhul* (God's curry), until I knew that it was made from different varieties of *xaak* like *bhedailota*, *manimuni* etc. In fact there is a *xaak* for almost every disease. Until about twenty-five years ago, people were totally dependant on their kitchen gardens for their daily supply of *xaak*.

Come *Bohag Bihu*, the Assamese New Year, the people just cannot have enough of different varieties of *xaak*. Traditionally, *xaak* is eaten on the seventh day of *Bihu*. But in some places, people have it on the second day of *Bohag Bihu* or even on the third. I prefer to have it on a Sunday.

Though people partake *saatxaaki* (seven varieties of *xaak*), depending upon the availability, the number may go up to as much as hundred and one varieties. Many varieties of wild *xaak* are also included here. It is a traditional Assamese belief that these *xaak* provide essential minerals, vitamins and nutrients required by the body. Some *xaak* which are otherwise toxic are believed to be rendered neutral by other varieties of *xaak*. If all one hundred and one varieties are unavailable, the ones which are available are cooked together along with the white tangy eggs of the *Aamruli porua* (a genus of the red tree ant) by some ethnic groups. The herbs are fried together in mustard oil.

The tender leaves of the following plants, leafy vegetables, shrubs or herbs can be eaten as *Saatxaaki*.

Assamese Name	English Name
Adamua	Chinese yam
Agora	Cocklebur
Alu	Potato
Amoi lota	Gulanch
Amora	Hog plum
Arahor	Pigeon pea
Arachan tita	Devil's pepper
Bakhor tita	Malabar nut
Bet gaj	Rattan cane
Bhedailota	King tonic
Bilati jetuka	Myrtle tree
Bonkapah	Firewood
Borkantaal urahi	Sword bean
Bor changoi tenga	Wood sorrel
Bon amlokhi	Emblica
Bon tulasi	Sweet basil
Chahpat	Tea leaf
Chal kumura	Ash gourd
China lai	Chinese cabbage
Chutia lofa	Buckwheat
Chagalee lota	Goat's foot creeper
Cirata	Wormwood
Dhania	Coriander leaves
Haati Khutura	Spiny amaranth
Ghora neem	Bead tree
Jani	Tymolseed

Assamese Name	English Name
Jani bon	Ironweed
Jaluk	Pepper
Jilmil xaak	Goosefoot
Jika	Ridge gourd
Jopa potari	Indian mallow
Joha kumura	Wax gourd
Kalmegh	King of bitter
Kantakari phal	Bitter brinjal
Katari dabua maah	Lima bean
Kath alu	White yam
Khecharee maah	Grass pea
Khoer	Clutch tree
Khutura	Green calalu
Kolmou	Swamp cabbage
Kon bilahi	Cherry tomato
Kopal phuta lota	Balloon vine
Korala	Scarlet gourd
Kotayan bengena	Horse nettle
Kuriyal	Orchid tree
Kuwari alu	Lisbon yam
Madar	Indian coral tree
Madhuri	Guava
Mahaneem	Margosa
Mithi	Fenugreek
Mitha alu	Sweet potato
Mula	Radish
Narasingha	Curry leaves
Olkasu	Elephant foot
Outenga	Elephant apple
Padina	Mint
Paleng	Spinach
Panilao	Bottlegourd
Pani kasu	Taro yam

Assamese Name	English Name
Pananua	Pigweed
Pokmou	Black nightshade
Rongalao	Pumpkin
Sajina	Drumstick
Saru changoi tenga	Creeping sorrel
Sauf	Fennel
Sewali phul	Coral jasmine
Sherata	Worm wood
Sugandhi lota	Parsely
Suka	Bladder dock
Tengesi	The Indian sorrel
Teteli	Tamarind
Titakerela	Bittergound
Titamora	Jute plant
Urahi	Butter bean

Assamese Name	Scientific Name
Bhat kerela	Momordica cochinchinensis
Bhekuri tita	Solanum violaceum
Bhringaraj	Spilanthes paniculata
Bih potal	Trichosanthes dioica
Bok phul	Sesbania grandi flora
Brahmi xaak	Bacopa monnieri
Chengmora	Lasia spinosa
Dhemesi xaak	Fagopyrum esculentum
Dhekia	Diplazium esculentum
Durun bon	Leucas linifolia
Hatisur	Heliotropium Indicum
Helechi	Enhydra fluctuans
Jatikhutura	Amaranthus viridus
Jutulipoka	Rubus moluccanus Linn
Keheraj	Eclipta prostrata Linn
Labarua	Rumex maritimus
Lai xaak	Malva verticillata
Laijabori	Drymaria cordata

Assamese Name	Scientific Name
Lehetibon	Hydrolea zeylanica
Maan dhania	Eryngium
Madhusuleng	Polygonum chinense
Malbhog xaak	Portulaca oleracea
Masundari	Houttuynia cordata
Mati fesua	Premna herbacea
Matikaduri	Alternanthera sessilis
Morolia	Stellaria media
Nefafu	Clerondendron colebrookianum
Pate gaja	Bryophyllum pinnatum
Puroi	Basella rubra
Sewali phul	Nyctanthes arbortristis
Tikani barua	Smilax perfoliata
Tita phul	Phlogacanthus tubiflorus
Tubuki lota	Cissampelos pareira
Zamlakhuti	Costus speciosus

Assamese Meals

Assamese cuisine is served in courses. A good meal can have seven courses. Every course served is always accompanied by a portion of rice. Normal rice or sticky rice is boiled, steamed or cooked in bamboo hollows. You can serve your choice of cooked rice with each of the following courses:

Lunch – 1
First course   Banana stem *khar* and baked fish in a banana leaf.
Second course   Yellow gram with drumstick leaves, fried bottlegourd and *kharisa*.
Third course   Duck curry with pumpkin fritters.
Fourth course   Elephant apple fish *tenga*.
Fifth course   *Payas* or curd.

Lunch – 2
First course   Herbs *khar*.
Second course   Moong daal with crushed ginger, mashed potatoes and mint chutney.
Third course   Mutton curry and cruncy brinjal fritters.
Fourth course   Chicken with bamboo shoot and a salad.
Fifth course   Steamed hilsa fish and *pani tenga*.
Sixth course   Tomato and *dhekia tenga*.
Seven course   Curd with jaggery.

Lunch – 3
First course   Fried fish guts and stuffed bittergourd.
Second course   Bengal gram with bamboo shoot, *dhekia*

Jyoti Das 231

	baked in a banana leaf, *pani tenga*, tomatoes and duck egg fry.
Third course	Curd fish and pumpkin flower fritters.
Fourth course	Fish curry with spinach.
Fifth course	Red lentil with elephant apples.
Sixth course	Rice powder *payas*.

Lunch – 4

First course	Papaya *khar*, mashed jackfruit seeds and mashed brinjal.
Second course	Fried *khutura*, fried fish, *kharisa* and moong dal with crushed ginger.
Third course	Pigeon curry.
Fourth course	Curd made of buffalo milk with jaggery.

Dinner – 1

First course	Jackfruit curry and Bengal gram with fermented bamboo shoot.
Second course	Drumstick with mustard seed paste and pumpkin fritters.
Third course	Fish kalia and *pani tenga*.
Fourth course	Chicken with ginger.
Fifth course	Potato *tenga* with cocum.
Sixth course	Sticky rice *payas*.

Dinner – 2

First course	Fish baked in bamboo hollows, fish with coconut juice and a chutney.
Second course	Mutton curry and a salad.
Third course	Chicken with bamboo shoot.
Fourth course	Red lentil with elephant apples.
Fifth course	Vanilla custard.

Dinner – 3
First course	Pork with split black gram and mashed brinjal
Second course	Boiled fish with rice powder and spadix fry.
Third course	Fermented bamboo shoot *tenga*.
Fourth course	Rice *payas*.

Dinner – 4
First course	Yellow gram with drumstick leaves, mixed vegetables and a chutney.
Second course	Mutton korma and cruncy brinjal fritters.
Third course	Chicken with pepper and *kharisa*.
Fourth course	Potato *tenga* with cocum.
Fifth course	Caramel pudding.

Dinner – 5
First course	Fish head with moong dal and baked fish in a banana leaf.
Second course	Steamed hilsa fish and fish egg pakoras.
Third course	Pigeon curry.
Fourth course	Elephant apple fish *tenga*.
Fifth course	Soft rice *payas*.

Glossary

English Name	Assamese Name
Almond	*badam*
Aniseed	*sauf*
Asafoetide	*hing*
Basil	*tulasi*
Bamboo shoot	*baanhgaaj*
Bay leaf	*tezpat*
Beaten rice	*chira*
Beet root	*beet*
Betel leaf	*pan*
Bengal gram	*butor dail*
Black gram	*mati dail*
Black pepper	*jaluk*
Bottlegourd	*panilao*
Broad bean	*urahi*
Butter	*makhan*
Cabbage	*bandhakobi*
Cardamom (black)	*bor elachi*
Cardamom (green)	*saru elachi*
Carrot	*gajar*
Cashewnut	*kaju*
Cauliflower	*phul kabi*
Chick peas	*kabuli boot*
Chicken	*kukura/murgi*
Chilli	*jalakia*
Chutney	*chutney*
Cinnamon	*daalcini*

Cloves	*long*
Club gourd	*bhul*
Colacasia	*kosu*
Coconut	*narikol*
Coriander	*dhania*
Corn	*makoi*
Cottage cheese	*paneer*
Cumin seed	*jeera*
Curd	*doi*
Curry leaf	*narasinghar pat*
Cucumber	*tiyah*
Dates	*khejur*
Dough	*mora atta*
Drumstick	*sajina*
Duck	*haanh*
Elephant apple	*outenga*
Essence	*sugandhi*
Fenugreek	*mithi*
Flour	*maida*
Fish	*maach*
Garlic	*nahoru*
Garnish	*sajua*
Ginger	*ada*
Gram flour	*besan*
Grapes	*angur*
Gravy	*jhul*
Green chilli	*kesa jalakia*
Green gram whole	*gota mogu*
Green gram	*mogur dail*
Green calalu	*khutura xaak*
Ice	*baraf*
Jaggery	*gur*
Kavai fruit	*kunduli*
Kidney beans	*rajma*
Lady's finger	*bhendi*

English Name	Assamese Name
Lemon	*kaji nemu*
Lentil	*masur dail*
Lettuce	*salad pat*
Lime	*golnemu*
Liver	*kalija*
Meat	*manxo*
Milk	*gakhir*
Mint leaves	*podina*
Molasses	*gur*
Mushroom	*kathphula*
Mustard	*sariah*
Mustard oil	*mitha tel*
Mutton	*chagoli manxo*
Nigella	*kaljeera*
Nutmeg	*jaaiphal*
Onion	*pyaj*
Papaya	*amita*
Parsely	*sugandhi lota*
Peas	*motor*
Pickle	*aachar*
Pigeon pea	*arahor dail*
Pistachio	*pista*
Poppy seed	*aaphu*
Prawn	*micha maach*
Pumpkin	*rongalao*
Radish	*moola*
Rind	*bakolee*
Rose water	*gulab jaal*
Sago	*sagu*
Saffron	*kesor*
Sesame seed	*til*
Semolina	*sooji*
Spinach	*paleng*

Sugar candy	*michiri*
Sweet	*mithai*
Sweet potato	*mitha alu*
Tamarind	*teteli*
Turmeric	*halodhi*
Vinegar	*chirika*
Walnut	*akhroot*
White yam	*kath alu*
Whey	*chana pani*
Yellow gram	*arahar dail*
Yeast	*khamer*

References

§ The Assamese fortnightly magazine *Prantik*

§ *Axomor Gos-Gosoni* by Sri Ananda Chandra Dutta

§ *Sahaj Loibbho Bon Dorobor Goon* by Dr Gunaram Khanikar

www.ingramcontent.com/pod-product-compliance
Lightning Source LLC
Chambersburg PA
CBHW031310150426
43191CD00005D/162